GUIDE BOOK FOR TOURIST

MELBOURNE
RESTAURANT GUIDE

RESTAURANTS, BARS AND CAFES
Your Guide to Authentic Regional Eats

GUIDE BOOK FOR TOURIST

MELBOURNE RESTAURANT GUIDE 2022
Best Rated Restaurants in Melbourne

© Arthur W. Groom
© E.G.P. Editorial

Printed in USA.

ISBN-13: 9798502692410

Copyright ©
All rights reserved.

MELBOURNE RESTAURANT GUIDE
The Most Recommended Restaurants in Melbourne

This directory is dedicated to Melbourne Business Owners and Managers who provide the experience that the locals and tourists enjoy. Thanks you very much for all that you do and thank for being the "People Choice".

Thanks to everyone that posts their reviews online and the amazing reviews sites that make our life easier.

The places listed in this book are the most positively reviewed and recommended by locals and travelers from around the world.

Thank you for your time and enjoy the directory that is designed with locals and tourist in mind!

TOP 500
RESTAURANTS
Ranked from #1 to #500

Melbourne Restaurant Guide / Restaurants, Bars & Cafés

#1
Movida Bar De Tapas
Cuisines: Spanish, Tapas
Average Price: Expensive
Area: Melbourne
Address: 1 Hosier Ln
Melbourne Victoria 3000
Phone: +61 3 9663 3038

#2
Bowery To Williamsburg
Cuisines: Deli, Coffee, Tea, American
Average Price: Modest
Area: Melbourne
Address: 18 Oliver Lane
Melbourne Victoria 3000
Phone: +61 3 9077 0162

#3
Cumulus Inc
Cuisines: Australian, Breakfast & Brunch
Average Price: Expensive
Area: Melbourne
Address: 45 Flinders Lane
Melbourne Victoria 3000
Phone: +61 3 9650 1445

#4
Chin Chin
Cuisines: Asian Fusion
Average Price: Modest
Area: Melbourne
Address: 125 Flinders La
Melbourne Victoria 3000
Phone: +61 3 8663 2000

#5
Brother Baba Budan
Cuisines: Café, Coffee, Tea
Average Price: Inexpensive
Area: Melbourne
Address: 359 Little Bourke St
Melbourne Victoria 3000
Phone: +61 3 9606 0449

#6
Izakaya Den
Cuisines: Japanese, Tapas
Average Price: Expensive
Area: Melbourne
Address: 114 Russell St
Melbourne Victoria 3000
Phone: +61 3 9654 2977

#7
The Hardware Societe
Cuisines: Breakfast & Brunch,
Spanish, French
Average Price: Modest
Area: Melbourne
Address: 120 Hardware St
Melbourne Victoria 3000
Phone: +61 3 9078 5992

#8
Vue De Monde
Cuisines: French, Australian, Bar
Average Price: Exclusive
Area: Melbourne
Address: 525 Collins St
Melbourne Victoria 3000
Phone: +61 3 9691 3888

#9
Captain Melville
Cuisines: Australian, Cocktail Bar,
Gastropub
Average Price: Modest
Area: Melbourne
Address: 34 Franklin St
Melbourne Victoria 3000
Phone: +61 3 9663 6855

#10
Nieuw Amsterdam
Cuisines: American, Cocktail Bar
Average Price: Expensive
Area: Melbourne
Address: 106-112 Hardware St
Melbourne Victoria 3000
Phone: +61 3 9602 111

#11
Mamak
Cuisines: Mamak
Average Price: Modest
Area: Melbourne
Address: 366 Lonsdale St
Melbourne Victoria 3000
Phone: +61 3 9670 3137

#12
Bomba
Cuisines: Tapas
Average Price: Modest
Area: Melbourne
Address: 103 Lonsdale St
Melbourne Victoria 3000
Phone: +61 3 9077 0451

#13
The Meatball & Wine Bar
Cuisines: Italian
Average Price: Modest
Area: Melbourne
Address: 135 Flinders Ln
Melbourne Victoria 3000
Phone: +61 3 9654 7545

#14
Coda
Cuisines: Vietnamese, Australian
Average Price: Expensive
Area: Melbourne
Address: 141 Flinders La
Melbourne Victoria 3000
Phone: +61 3 9650 3155

#15
Mr Burger
Cuisines: Burgers
Average Price: Inexpensive
Area: Melbourne
Address: 93 Therry St
Melbourne Victoria 3000
Phone: +61 3 9329 7304

#16
GAZI
Cuisines: Greek, European
Average Price: Expensive
Area: Melbourne
Address: 2 Exhibition St
Melbourne Victoria 3000
Phone: +61 3 9677 9677

#17
Gami Little Lonsdale
Cuisines: Korean, Chicken Shop
Average Price: Modest
Area: Melbourne
Address: 100 Little Lonsdale St
Melbourne Victoria 3000
Phone: +61 3 9671 3232

#18
Sakura Kaiten
Cuisines: Sushi Bar, Japanese
Average Price: Modest
Area: Melbourne
Address: 61 Little Collins St
Melbourne Victoria 3000
Phone: +61 3 9663 0898

#19
Miss Chu
Cuisines: Vietnamese, Asian Fusion
Average Price: Modest
Area: Melbourne
Address: 297 Exhibition St
Melbourne Victoria 3000
Phone: +61 3 9077 1097

#20
Seamstress
Cuisines: Bar, Asian Fusion
Average Price: Expensive
Area: Melbourne
Address: 113 Lonsdale St
Melbourne Victoria 3000
Phone: +61 3 9663 6363

#21
Maha
Cuisines: Middle Eastern, Cocktail Bar
Average Price: Exclusive
Area: Melbourne
Address: 21 Bond St
Melbourne Victoria 3000
Phone: +61 3 9629 5900

#22
The Grain Store
Cuisines: Australian, Breakfast & Brunch
Average Price: Modest
Area: Melbourne
Address: 517 Flinders Lane
Melbourne Victoria 3000
Phone: +61 3 9972 6993

#23
Movida Aqui
Cuisines: Tapas, Spanish
Average Price: Expensive
Area: Melbourne
Address: 500 Bourke St
Melbourne Victoria 3000
Phone: +61 3 9663 3038

#24
Shandong Mama
Cuisines: Chinese
Average Price: Inexpensive
Area: Melbourne
Address: 200 Bourke St, Mid City Arcade
Melbourne Victoria 3000
Phone: +61 3 9650 3818

#25
Trunk
Cuisines: Bar, Mediterranean, Burgers
Average Price: Modest
Area: Melbourne
Address: 275 Exhibition St
Melbourne Victoria 3000
Phone: +61 3 9663 7994

#26
Kinfolk
Cuisines: Café
Average Price: Inexpensive
Area: Melbourne
Address: 673 Bourke St
Melbourne Victoria 3000
Phone: +61 4 2322 9953

#27
Manchester Press
Cuisines: Café, Coffee, Tea, Breakfast & Brunch, Sandwiches
Average Price: Inexpensive
Area: Melbourne
Address: 8 Rankins Lane
Melbourne Victoria 3000
Phone: +61 3 9600 4054

#28
Cumulus Up
Cuisines: Wine Bar, Australian
Average Price: Expensive
Area: Melbourne
Address: 28-66 Flinders Ln
Melbourne Victoria 3000
Phone: +61 3 9650 1445

#29
La Belle Miette
Cuisines: Desserts, French, Bakery
Average Price: Inexpensive
Area: Melbourne
Address: 30 Hardware Lane
Melbourne Victoria 3000
Phone: +61 3 9024 4528

#30
Red Spice Road
Cuisines: Bar, Asian Fusion, Thai
Average Price: Expensive
Area: Melbourne
Address: 27 Mckillop St
Melbourne Victoria 3000
Phone: +61 3 9603 1601

#31
Shanghai St
Cuisines: Shanghainese
Average Price: Inexpensive
Area: Melbourne
Address: 342 Little Bourke St
Melbourne Victoria 3000
Phone: +61 3 9600 2250

#32
The Melbourne Supper Club
Cuisines: Wine Bar, Tapas
Average Price: Expensive
Area: Melbourne
Address: 161 Spring St
Melbourne Victoria 3000
Phone: +61 3 9654 6300

#33
Bistro Vue
Cuisines: French
Average Price: Inexpensive
Area: Melbourne
Address: 430 Little Collins St
Melbourne Victoria 3000
Phone: +61 3 9691 3838

#34
1806
Cuisines: Lounge, Tapas, Cocktail Bar
Average Price: Modest
Area: Melbourne
Address: 169 Exhibition St
Melbourne Victoria 3000
Phone: +61 3 9663 7722

#35
Fatto
Cuisines: Italian, Café
Average Price: Expensive
Area: Southbank
Address: 100 St Kilda Road
Melbourne Victoria 3004
Phone: +61 3 8698 8800

#36
Murmur Bar
Cuisines: Tapas, Lounge
Average Price: Expensive
Area: Melbourne
Address: 17 Warburton Ln
Melbourne Victoria 3000
Phone: +61 3 9640 0395

#37
Mamasita
Cuisines: Mexican, Tapas
Average Price: Expensive
Area: Melbourne
Address: 11 Collins St
Melbourne Victoria 3000
Phone: +61 3 9650 3821

#38
Movida Next Door
Cuisines: Spanish, Tapas
Average Price: Modest
Area: Melbourne
Address: 164 Flinders St
Melbourne Victoria 3000
Phone: +61 3 9663 3038

#39
Nam Loong Chinese Restaurant
Cuisines: Chinese
Average Price: Inexpensive
Area: Melbourne
Address: 223 Russell St
Melbourne Victoria 3000
Phone: +61 3 9663 4089

#40
Taxi Kitchen
Cuisines: Gluten-Free, European, Japanese
Average Price: Exclusive
Area: Melbourne
Address: Federation Sq
Melbourne Victoria 3067
Phone: +61 3 9654 8808

#41
Papa Goose
Cuisines: British, Cocktail Bar
Average Price: Expensive
Area: Melbourne
Address: 91 Flinders Ln
Melbourne Victoria 3000
Phone: +61 3 9663 2800

#42
Solarino
Cuisines: Italian
Average Price: Modest
Area: Melbourne
Address: Shop 7, 279 Little Collins St
Melbourne Victoria 3000
Phone: +61 3 9663 2636

#43
Cookie
Cuisines: Thai, Cocktail Bar
Average Price: Modest
Area: Melbourne
Address: 252 Swanston St
Melbourne Victoria 3000
Phone: +61 3 9663 7660

#44
Chuckle Park
Cuisines: Bar, Café
Average Price: Modest
Area: Melbourne
Address: 322 Little Collins St
Melbourne Victoria 3000
Phone: +61 3 9650 4494

#45
EARL Canteen
Cuisines: Sandwiches, Breakfast & Brunch, Fast Food
Average Price: Inexpensive
Area: Melbourne
Address: 500 Bourke St
Melbourne Victoria 3000
Phone: +61 3 9600 1995

#46
Longrain Restaurant & Bar
Cuisines: Thai, Australian
Average Price: Expensive
Area: Melbourne
Address: 40-44 Little Bourke St
Melbourne Victoria 3000
Phone: +61 3 9671 3151

#47
Tonka
Cuisines: Indian, Australian
Average Price: Expensive
Area: Melbourne
Address: 20 Duckboard Pl
Melbourne Victoria 3000
Phone: +61 9 6503 155

#48
Gingerboy
Cuisines: Asian Fusion
Average Price: Expensive
Area: Melbourne
Address: 27-29 Crossley St
Melbourne Victoria 3000
Phone: +61 3 9662 4200

#49
Operator25
Cuisines: Breakfast & Brunch, Café, Tea
Average Price: Modest
Area: Melbourne
Address: 25 Wills St
Melbourne Victoria 3000
Phone: +61 3 9670 3278

#50
The League Of Honest Coffee
Cuisines: Café, Coffee, Tea
Average Price: Inexpensive
Area: Melbourne
Address: 8 Exploration Ln
Melbourne Victoria 3000
Phone: +61 3 9654 0169

#51
Curtin House Rooftop Bar
Cuisines: Bar, Restaurant, Music Venues
Average Price: Modest
Area: Melbourne
Address: 252 Swanston St
Melbourne Victoria 3000
Phone: +61 3 9654 5394

#52
Supernormal
Cuisines: Asian Fusion, Tapas
Average Price: Expensive
Area: Melbourne
Address: 180 Flinders Ln
Melbourne Victoria 3000
Phone: +61 3 9650 8688

#53
Yamato Japanese Restaurant
Cuisines: Japanese
Average Price: Modest
Area: Melbourne
Address: 28 Corrs Lane
Melbourne Victoria 3000
Phone: +61 3 9663 1706

#54
The Workshop Bar
Cuisines: Bar, Café, Gastropub
Average Price: Inexpensive
Area: Melbourne
Address: 413 Elizabeth St
Melbourne Victoria 3000
Phone: +61 3 9326 4365

#55
Henry And The Fox
Cuisines: European
Average Price: Modest
Area: Melbourne
Address: Corner Of Little Collins
& Mccrackens Ln Melbourne Victoria 3000
Phone: +61 3 9614 3277

#56
+39 Pizzeria
Cuisines: Pizza, Italian
Average Price: Modest
Area: Melbourne
Address: 362 Little Bourke St
Melbourne Victoria 3000
Phone: +61 3 9642 0440

#57
Purple Peanuts
Cuisines: Japanese, Sushi Bar
Average Price: Inexpensive
Area: Melbourne
Address: 620 Collins St
Melbourne Victoria 3000
Phone: +61 3 9620 9548

#58
De Alleyway Espresso
Cuisines: Café, Desserts, Coffee, Tea
Average Price: Inexpensive
Area: Melbourne
Address: 318-322 Little Collins St
Melbourne Victoria 3000
Phone: +61 4 1121 3211

#59
Il Solito Posto
Cuisines: Italian
Average Price: Modest
Area: Melbourne
Address: 113 Collins St
Melbourne Victoria 3000
Phone: +61 3 9654 4466

#60
Stalactites
Cuisines: Greek
Average Price: Modest
Area: Melbourne
Address: 183 Lonsdale St
Melbourne Victoria 3000
Phone: +61 3 9663 3316

#61
Bottega Restaurant
Cuisines: Italian
Average Price: Modest
Area: Melbourne
Address: 74 Bourke St
Melbourne Victoria 3000
Phone: +61 3 9654 2252

#62
Pellegrini's
Cuisines: Italian, Café
Average Price: Inexpensive
Area: Melbourne
Address: 66 Bourke St
Melbourne Victoria 3000
Phone: +61 3 9662 1885

#63
Saké
Cuisines: Japanese
Average Price: Expensive
Area: Southbank
Address: 100 St Kilda Rd
Melbourne Victoria 3004
Phone: +61 3 8687 0775

#64
Shimbashi Soba & Sake Bar
Cuisines: Japanese
Average Price: Modest
Area: Melbourne
Address: 17 Liverpool St
Melbourne Victoria 3000
Phone: +61 3 9654 6727

#65
Amigos
Cuisines: Mexican
Average Price: Modest
Area: Melbourne
Address: 75 Hardware Ln
Melbourne Victoria 3000
Phone: +61 3 9670 7797

#66
Little Ramen Bar
Cuisines: Ramen, Café
Average Price: Inexpensive
Area: Melbourne
Address: 346 Little Bourke St
Melbourne Victoria 3000
Phone: +61 3 9670 5558

#67
Filter
Cuisines: Coffee, Tea, Scandinavian
Average Price: Inexpensive
Area: Melbourne
Address: 555 Collins St
Melbourne Victoria 3000
Phone: +61 3 9620 1211

#68
Darac
Cuisines: Japanese, Korean
Average Price: Modest
Area: Melbourne
Address: 53 A'Beckett St
Melbourne Victoria 3000
Phone: +61 3 9662 2441

#69
Sichuan House
Cuisines: Szechuan
Average Price: Modest
Area: Melbourne
Address: 22-26 Corrs La
Melbourne Victoria 3000
Phone: +61 3 9650 8589

#70
King's Steak & Seafood Bar
Cuisines: Seafood, Steakhouse
Average Price: Modest
Area: Melbourne
Address: 209 King St
Melbourne Victoria 3000
Phone: +61 3 9602 1213

#71
The Quarter
Cuisines: Café, European
Average Price: Modest
Area: Melbourne
Address: 27-31 Degraves St
Melbourne Victoria 3000
Phone: +61 3 9650 6156

#72
Riverland Bar
Cuisines: Café, Bar, European
Average Price: Modest
Area: Melbourne
Address: Vaults 1-9 Federation Whrf
Melbourne Victoria 3000
Phone: +61 3 9662 1771

#73
Añada
Cuisines: Spanish, Tapas
Average Price: Expensive
Area: Fitzroy
Address: 197 Gertrude St
Melbourne Victoria 3065
Phone: +61 3 9415 6101

#74
Laksa Bar
Cuisines: Malaysian
Average Price: Inexpensive
Area: Melbourne
Address: 108 Little Lonsdale St
Melbourne Victoria 3000
Phone: +61 3 9663 1941

#75
Gill's Diner
Cuisines: European
Average Price: Expensive
Area: Melbourne
Address: 360 Little Collins St
Melbourne Victoria 3000
Phone: +61 3 9670 7214

#76
Ezard
Cuisines: Venues, Event Space
Average Price: Exclusive
Area: Melbourne
Address: 187 Flinders Ln
Melbourne Victoria 3000
Phone: +61 3 9639 6811

#77
Cabinet
Cuisines: European, Tapas, Bar
Average Price: Modest
Area: Melbourne
Address: 11 Rainbow Alley
Melbourne Victoria 3000
Phone: +61 3 9654 0915

#78
Nama Nama
Cuisines: Japanese, Sushi Bar
Average Price: Modest
Area: Melbourne
Address: 31 Spring St
Melbourne Victoria 3000
Phone: +61 3 9639 9500

#79
Prime House
Cuisines: Burgers, Sandwiches, Breakfast & Brunch
Average Price: Modest
Area: Melbourne
Address: 500 Bourke St
Melbourne Victoria 3000
Phone: +61 3 9602 2955

#80
Schnitz Pan Cooked Schnitzels
Cuisines: Australian
Average Price: Inexpensive
Area: Melbourne
Address: 203-207 Elizabeth St
Melbourne Victoria 3000
Phone: +61 3 9606 0388

#81
Maccaroni Trattoria Italiana
Cuisines: Italian, Coffee, Tea
Average Price: Modest
Area: Melbourne
Address: 10 Manchester La
Melbourne Victoria 3000
Phone: +61 3 9090 7634

#82
Big Boy BBQ
Cuisines: American
Average Price: Modest
Area: Melbourne
Address: 27-31 Hardware Ln
Melbourne Victoria 3000
Phone: +61 3 9670 9388

#83
Pho Dzung City Noodle Shop
Cuisines: Restaurant
Average Price: Inexpensive
Area: Melbourne
Address: 234 Russell St
Melbourne Victoria 3000
Phone: +61 3 9663 8885

#84
Mekong Vietnam
Cuisines: Soup, Vietnamese
Average Price: Inexpensive
Area: Melbourne
Address: 241 Swanston St
Melbourne Victoria 3000
Phone: +61 3 9663 3288

#85
Tokui Sushi
Cuisines: Sushi Bar, Japanese
Average Price: Inexpensive
Area: Melbourne
Address: 260 Lonsdale St
Melbourne Victoria 3000
Phone: +61 3 9663 9966

#86
Hofbräuhaus
Cuisines: German
Average Price: Modest
Area: Melbourne
Address: 24-26 Market Lane
Melbourne Victoria 3000
Phone: +61 3 9663 3361

#87
Don Don
Cuisines: Japanese, Fast Food
Average Price: Inexpensive
Area: Melbourne
Address: 198 Little Lonsdale St
Melbourne Victoria 3000
Phone: +61 3 9670 7113

#88
Pho & Co
Cuisines: Vietnamese, Asian Fusion
Average Price: Modest
Area: Melbourne
Address: 122 Russell St
Melbourne Victoria 3000
Phone: +61 3 9654 5923

#89
Great Eastern Groceries Centre
Cuisines: Grocery, Ethnic Food, Chinese
Average Price: Inexpensive
Area: Melbourne
Address: 185- 187 Russell St
Melbourne Victoria 3000
Phone: +61 3 9663 3716

#90
San Telmo
Cuisines: Argentine
Average Price: Expensive
Area: Melbourne
Address: 14 Meyers Pl
Melbourne Victoria 3000
Phone: +61 3 9650 5525

#91
Guhng The Palace
Cuisines: Korean, Asian Fusion
Average Price: Modest
Area: Melbourne
Address: 19 Mckillop St
Melbourne Victoria 3000
Phone: +61 3 9041 2192

#92
Spicy Fish
Cuisines: Chinese
Average Price: Modest
Area: Melbourne
Address: 209 Little Bourke St
Melbourne Victoria 3000
Phone: +61 3 9639 1885

#93
Om Vegetarian
Cuisines: Indian, Vegetarian
Average Price: Inexpensive
Area: Melbourne
Address: 28 Elizabeth St
Melbourne Victoria 3000
Phone: +61 3 9663 0062

#94
La Petite Crêperie
Cuisines: Desserts, Crêperie, St Vendor
Average Price: Inexpensive
Area: Melbourne
Address: Cnr Swanston And Little Collins St
Melbourne Victoria 3000
Phone: +61 4 0400 2341

#95
Curry Vault Indian Restaurant & Bar
Cuisines: Indian
Average Price: Modest
Area: Melbourne
Address: 18-20 Bank Pl
Melbourne Victoria 3000
Phone: +61 3 9600 0144

#96
Hare And Grace
Cuisines: Australian
Average Price: Expensive
Area: Melbourne
Address: 525 Collins St
Melbourne Victoria 3000
Phone: +61 3 9629 6755

#97
Cajun Kitchen
Cuisines: Café
Average Price: Modest
Area: Melbourne
Address: 136 Elizabeth St
Melbourne Victoria 3000
Phone: +61 3 9663 8816

#98
Blok M Express
Cuisines: Indonesian
Average Price: Inexpensive
Area: Melbourne
Address: 380 Little Bourke St
Melbourne Victoria 3000
Phone: +61 3 9600 2534

#99
Tadka Boom!
Cuisines: Indian
Average Price: Inexpensive
Area: Melbourne
Address: 550 Bourke St
Melbourne Victoria 3000
Phone: +61 3 9600 1633

#100
Grill'd Healthy Burgers
Cuisines: Burgers, Fast Food
Average Price: Modest
Area: Melbourne
Address: Level 3
Melbourne Central
Melbourne Victoria 3000
Phone: +61 3 9663 0399

#101
Bomba Rooftop
Cuisines: Bar, Spanish
Average Price: Modest
Area: Melbourne
Address: 103 Lonsdale St
Melbourne Victoria 3000
Phone: +61 3 9077 0451

#102
Mister Close
Cuisines: Café
Average Price: Modest
Area: Melbourne
Address: 246 Bourke St
Melbourne Victoria 3000
Phone: +61 3 9654 7778

#103
Yamato
Cuisines: Japanese
Average Price: Inexpensive
Area: Melbourne
Address: 223 Exhibition St
Melbourne Victoria 3000
Phone: +61 3 9663 1707

#104
Collins Quarter
Cuisines: Hotel, Bar, Gastropub
Average Price: Expensive
Area: Melbourne
Address: 86A Collins St
Melbourne Victoria 3000
Phone: +61 3 9650 8500

#105
Crossways
Cuisines: Vegetarian, Asian Fusion
Average Price: Inexpensive
Area: Melbourne
Address: 123 Swanston St
Melbourne Victoria 3000
Phone: +61 3 9650 2939

#106
Fonda Mexican
Cuisines: Mexican
Average Price: Modest
Area: Melbourne
Address: 31 Flinders Ln
Melbourne Victoria 3000
Phone: +61 3 8686 7300

#107
Moat
Cuisines: European
Average Price: Expensive
Area: Melbourne
Address: 176 Little Lonsdale St
Melbourne Victoria 3000
Phone: +61 3 9094 7820

#108
Old Beijing Dumpling Restaurant
Cuisines: Chinese
Average Price: Inexpensive
Area: Melbourne
Address: 270 Flinders St
Melbourne Victoria 3000
Phone: +61 3 9663 6036

#109
Threefold, Food Store & Eatery
Cuisines: Café
Average Price: Modest
Area: Melbourne
Address: 381 Flinders Lane
Melbourne Victoria 3000
Phone: +61 3 9614 8194

#110
Milky Joe's
Cuisines: Café
Average Price: Inexpensive
Area: Melbourne
Address: 210 Lonsdale St
Melbourne Victoria 3000
Phone: +61 3 9663 3613

#111
Izakaya Chuji
Cuisines: Sushi Bar, Izakaya
Average Price: Modest
Area: Melbourne
Address: 165 Lonsdale St
Melbourne Victoria 3000
Phone: +61 3 9663 8118

#112
Fomo Thai
Cuisines: Thai
Average Price: Modest
Area: Melbourne
Address: 171 Bourke St
Melbourne Victoria 3000
Phone: +61 3 9650 7987

#113
Brooks Of Melbourne
Cuisines: Australian, Bar
Average Price: Expensive
Area: Melbourne
Address: 115-117 Collins St
Melbourne Victoria 3000
Phone: +61 3 9001 8755

#114
Oli & Levi
Cuisines: Café
Average Price: Inexpensive
Area: Melbourne
Address: 20 Coromandel Pl
Melbourne Victoria 3000
Phone: +61 3 9650 0501

#115
Pei Modern
Cuisines: Australian, French
Average Price: Expensive
Area: Melbourne
Address: 45 Collins St
Melbourne Victoria 3000
Phone: +61 3 9654 8545

#116
Portello Rosso Tapas & Jamon Bar
Cuisines: Spanish
Average Price: Expensive
Area: Melbourne
Address: 15 Warburton Ln
Melbourne Victoria 3000
Phone: +61 3 9602 2273

#117
Sahara Restaurant
Cuisines: Moroccan
Average Price: Inexpensive
Area: Melbourne
Address: 301 Swanston Wlk
Melbourne Victoria 3000
Phone: +61 3 9663 8477

#118
Issus
Cuisines: Café, European, Breakfast & Brunch
Average Price: Modest
Area: Melbourne
Address: 8-10 Centre Pl
Melbourne Victoria 3000
Phone: +61 3 9663 8844

#119
Kokoro Ramen
Cuisines: Japanese
Average Price: Inexpensive
Area: Melbourne
Address: 157 Lonsdale St
Melbourne Victoria 3000
Phone: +61 3 9650 1215

#120
Gyoza Douraku
Cuisines: Japanese
Average Price: Modest
Area: Melbourne
Address: 147 Bourke St
Melbourne Victoria 3000
Phone: +61 3 9650 5225

#121
Charles Dickens Tavern Melbourne
Cuisines: Pub, British
Average Price: Modest
Area: Melbourne
Address: 290 Collins St
Melbourne Victoria 3000
Phone: +61 3 9654 1821

#122
Mrs Parma's
Cuisines: Pub, Parma
Average Price: Modest
Area: Melbourne
Address: 25 Little Bourke St
Melbourne Victoria 3000
Phone: +61 3 9639 2269

#123
Grill'd Healthy Burgers
Cuisines: Burgers, Vegetarian, Fast Food
Average Price: Modest
Area: Melbourne
Address: 15 Degraves St
Melbourne Victoria 3000
Phone: +61 3 9654 7666

#124
The European
Cuisines: Wine Bar, French, Italian
Average Price: Expensive
Area: Melbourne
Address: 161 Spring St
Melbourne Victoria 3000
Phone: +61 3 9654 0811

#125
Don Too
Cuisines: Japanese, Sushi Bar, Food
Average Price: Inexpensive
Area: Melbourne
Address: 330 Little Lonsdale St
Melbourne Victoria 3000
Phone: +61 3 9670 7113

#126
Pok Pok Jnr
Cuisines: Coffee, Tea, Thai
Average Price: Inexpensive
Area: Melbourne
Address: 555 Bourke St
Melbourne Victoria 3000
Phone: +61 3 9629 5881

#127
Gordon's Cafe
Cuisines: Coffee, Tea, Breakfast & Brunch
Average Price: Modest
Area: Melbourne
Address: 304-306 Little Collins St
Melbourne Victoria 3000
Phone: +61 3 9663 5103

#128
Hanaichi Japanese
Cuisines: Japanese
Average Price: Inexpensive
Area: Melbourne
Address: 13 QV Sq
Melbourne Victoria 3000
Phone: +61 3 9662 9409

#129
Hutong Dumpling Bar
Cuisines: Chinese
Average Price: Modest
Area: Melbourne
Address: 14-16 Market Ln
Melbourne Victoria 3000
Phone: +61 3 9650 8128

#130
Ombra Salumi Bar
Cuisines: Italian
Average Price: Modest
Area: Melbourne
Address: 76 Bourke St
Melbourne Victoria 3000
Phone: +61 3 9639 1927

#131
Ruyi Dumpling & Wine Bar
Cuisines: Asian Fusion, Chinese, Wine Bar
Average Price: Modest
Area: Melbourne
Address: 16 Liverpoole St
Melbourne Victoria 3000
Phone: +61 3 9090 7778

#132
Robot
Cuisines: Bar, Japanese, Sushi Bar
Average Price: Modest
Area: Melbourne
Address: 12 Bligh Pl
Melbourne Victoria 3000
Phone: +61 3 9620 3646

#133
Flower Drum
Cuisines: Chinese
Average Price: Exclusive
Area: Melbourne
Address: 17 Market Ln
Melbourne Victoria 3000
Phone: +61 3 9662 3655

#134
Bar Lourinhã
Cuisines: Bar, Tapas, Mediterranean
Average Price: Modest
Area: Melbourne
Address: 37 Little Collins St
Melbourne Victoria 3000
Phone: +61 3 9663 7890

#135
Bali Bagus
Cuisines: Halal, Indonesian
Average Price: Inexpensive
Area: Melbourne
Address: U707/ 85 Franklin St
Melbourne Victoria 3000
Phone: +61 3 9662 1474

#136
Little King Cafe
Cuisines: Coffee, Tea, Café
Average Price: Inexpensive
Area: Melbourne
Address: Shp4/ 209 Flinders Rd
Melbourne Victoria 3000
Phone: +61 3 9654 0030

#137
Red Silks
Cuisines: Chinese, Malaysian
Average Price: Modest
Area: Melbourne
Address: Level 1, 200 Bourke St
Melbourne Victoria 3000
Phone: +61 3 9663 9922

#138
Beer Deluxe
Cuisines: Burgers, Beer Bar, Pizza
Average Price: Modest
Area: Melbourne
Address: Federation Sq
Melbourne Victoria 3000
Phone: +61 3 9663 0166

#139
B'Churrasco
Cuisines: Brazilian
Average Price: Modest
Area: Melbourne
Address: 61 A'Beckett St
Melbourne Victoria 3000
Phone: +61 3 8060 4770

#140
Market Lane Coffee
Cuisines: Café, Coffee, Tea
Average Price: Inexpensive
Area: Melbourne
Address: 109-111 Therry St
Melbourne Victoria 3000
Phone: +61 3 9326 8341

#141
Mad Mex
Cuisines: Mexican
Average Price: Inexpensive
Area: Melbourne
Address: QV - Red Cape Lane
Melbourne Victoria 3000
Phone: +61 3 9662 3002

#142
Toby's Estate
Cuisines: Coffee, Tea, Breakfast & Brunch
Average Price: Inexpensive
Area: Melbourne
Address: 325 Flinders Ln
Melbourne Victoria 3000
Phone: +61 3 9939 4578

#143
Dainty Sichuan Food
Cuisines: Szechuan
Average Price: Modest
Area: Melbourne
Address: 206 Bourke St
Melbourne Victoria 3000
Phone: +61 3 9650 2188

#144
Dolan Uyghur Food Heaven
Cuisines: Halal, Chinese, Turkish
Average Price: Inexpensive
Area: Melbourne
Address: 166 Little Lonsdale St
Melbourne Victoria 3000
Phone: +61 4 3384 2123

#145
Turf Bar
Cuisines: Sports Bar, Steakhouse, Pizza
Average Price: Expensive
Area: Melbourne
Address: 131 Queen St
Melbourne Victoria 3000
Phone: +61 3 9670 1271

#146
Little Bean Blue
Cuisines: Café, Coffee, Tea
Average Price: Inexpensive
Area: Melbourne
Address: 15 Little Collins St
Melbourne Victoria 3000
Phone: +61 3 9650 0046

#147
Madamimadam
Cuisines: Coffee, Tea, Australian
Average Price: Inexpensive
Area: Melbourne
Address: 16 Equitable Pl
Melbourne Victoria 3000
Phone: +61 3 9600 2506

#148
Coconut House
Cuisines: Malaysian, Chinese
Average Price: Inexpensive
Area: Melbourne
Address: 449 Elizabeth St
Melbourne Victoria 3000
Phone: +61 3 9329 6401

#149
Classic Curry
Cuisines: Indian
Average Price: Inexpensive
Area: Melbourne
Address: 597 Elizabeth St
Melbourne Victoria 3000
Phone: +61 3 9329 4040

#150
Bistrot d'Orsay
Cuisines: French
Average Price: Expensive
Area: Melbourne
Address: 184 Collins St
Melbourne Victoria 3000
Phone: +61 3 9654 6498

#151
Campari House
Cuisines: Bar, European
Average Price: Modest
Area: Melbourne
Address: 23 Hardware Ln
Melbourne Victoria 3000
Phone: +61 3 9600 1574

#152
Mr Burger
Cuisines: Burgers, Food Truck
Average Price: Inexpensive
Area: Melbourne
Address: 428 Little Bourke St
Melbourne Victoria 3000
Phone: +61 3 9329 7304

#153
Ca De Vin
Cuisines: Café, Italian, Mediterranean
Average Price: Modest
Area: Melbourne
Address: Postal Ln
Melbourne Victoria 3003
Phone: +61 3 9654 3639

#154
American Doughnut Kitchen
Cuisines: Restaurant
Average Price: Inexpensive
Area: Melbourne
Address: Queen Victoria Market,
Cnr Queen & Therry Sts
Melbourne Victoria 3000
Phone: +61 4 4887 7719

#155
Red Spice Road QV
Cuisines: Asian Fusion, Vietnamese, Thai
Average Price: Exclusive
Area: Melbourne
Address: 31-37 Artemis Ln QV
Melbourne Victoria 3000
Phone: +61 3 8660 6300

#156
The Carlton Hotel
Cuisines: Gastropub, Pub
Average Price: Modest
Area: Melbourne
Address: 193 Bourke St
Melbourne Victoria 3000
Phone: +61 3 9663 3246

#157
Rice Paper Scissors
Cuisines: Asian Fusion, Vietnamese
Average Price: Modest
Area: Melbourne
Address: 19 Liverpool St
Melbourne Victoria 3000
Phone: +61 3 9663 9890

#158
Cafe No 5
Cuisines: Café
Average Price: Inexpensive
Area: Melbourne
Address: 5 Centre Pl
Melbourne Victoria 3000
Phone: +61 3 9650 0055

#159
Non Solo Pasta NSP
Cuisines: Café, Italian
Average Price: Modest
Area: Docklands
Address: 800 Collins St
Melbourne Victoria 3000
Phone: +61 3 9620 1110

#160
Roule Galette
Cuisines: French, Crêperie, Desserts
Average Price: Modest
Area: Melbourne
Address: 241 Flinders Ln
Melbourne Victoria 3000
Phone: +61 3 9639 0307

#161
Mr Mason
Cuisines: French
Average Price: Expensive
Area: Melbourne
Address: 530 Collins St
Melbourne Victoria 3000
Phone: +61 3 9614 4500

#162
La Chinesca
Cuisines: Asian Fusion
Average Price: Modest
Area: Melbourne
Address: 71 Collins St
Melbourne Victoria 3000
Phone: +61 3 9663 8333

#163
Yu-U
Cuisines: Japanese
Average Price: Modest
Area: Melbourne
Address: 137 Flinders Lane
Melbourne Victoria 3000
Phone: +61 3 9639 7073

#164
Hairy Canary
Cuisines: Spanish, Bar
Average Price: Modest
Area: Melbourne
Address: 212 Little Collins St
Melbourne Victoria 3000
Phone: +61 3 9654 2471

#165
T-Roy Browns
Cuisines: Restaurant, Coffee, Tea
Average Price: Inexpensive
Area: Melbourne
Address: Banana Alley
Melbourne Victoria 3000
Phone: +61 4 2148 9588

#166
Aix Café Creperie Salon
Cuisines: Crêperie, French, Desserts
Average Price: Inexpensive
Area: Melbourne
Address: 24 Centre Pl
Melbourne Victoria 3000
Phone: +61 3 9662 2667

#167
La Citta
Cuisines: Restaurant
Average Price: Expensive
Area: Melbourne
Address: 11 Degraves St
Melbourne Victoria 3000
Phone: +61 3 9014 8824

#168
Hako Japenese Restaurant & Bar
Cuisines: Japanese
Average Price: Modest
Area: Melbourne
Address: 310 Flinders Lane
Melbourne Victoria 3000
Phone: +61 3 9620 1881

#169
Vicolino
Cuisines: Café
Average Price: Modest
Area: Melbourne
Address: 17 Centre Pl
Melbourne Victoria 3000
Phone: +61 3 9650 1855

#170
Hibachi
Cuisines: Japanese, Sushi Bar
Average Price: Modest
Area: Melbourne
Address: 228 King St
Melbourne Victoria 3000
Phone: +61 3 9670 1661

#171
Fukuryu Ramen
Cuisines: Japanese, Asian Fusion
Average Price: Inexpensive
Area: Melbourne
Address: 22 Corrs Ln
Melbourne Victoria 3000
Phone: +61 3 9090 7149

#172
Brutale 2.0
Cuisines: Eastern European, Bar, Pub Food
Average Price: Expensive
Area: Melbourne
Address: 18 Corrs Lane
Melbourne Victoria 3000
Phone: +61 3 9654 4411

#173
Tuscan Bar
Cuisines: Italian
Average Price: Modest
Area: Melbourne
Address: 79 Bourke St
Melbourne Victoria 3000
Phone: +61 3 9671 3322

#174
Yak Italian Kitchen
Cuisines: Italian
Average Price: Modest
Area: Melbourne
Address: 150 Flinders Lane
Melbourne Victoria 3000
Phone: +61 3 9654 6699

#175
Grasshopper's Feast
Cuisines: Café
Average Price: Modest
Area: Melbourne
Address: The Causeway
Melbourne Victoria 3000
Phone: +61 3 9663 8404

#176
Cecconi's Flinders Lane
Cuisines: Italian, Gluten-Free, Vegetarian
Average Price: Exclusive
Area: Melbourne
Address: 61 Flinders Ln
Melbourne Victoria 3000
Phone: +61 3 8663 0500

#177
Touché Hombre
Cuisines: Mexican, Latin American
Average Price: Modest
Area: Melbourne
Address: 233 Lonsdale St
Melbourne Victoria 3000
Phone: +61 3 9663 0811

#178
Oriental Spoon
Cuisines: Korean
Average Price: Modest
Area: Melbourne
Address: 254 La Trobe St
Melbourne Victoria 3000
Phone: +61 3 9654 9930

#179
Famish'd
Cuisines: Café, Coffee, Tea, Breakfast & Brunch
Average Price: Inexpensive
Area: Melbourne
Address: 130 Little Collins St
Melbourne Victoria 3000
Phone: +61 3 9004 0322

#180
Shanghai Village
Cuisines: Shanghainese
Average Price: Inexpensive
Area: Melbourne
Address: 112 Little Bourke St
Melbourne Victoria 3000
Phone: +61 3 9663 1878

#181
Noodle Kingdom
Cuisines: Chinese
Average Price: Modest
Area: Melbourne
Address: 175 Russell St
Melbourne Victoria 3000
Phone: +61 3 9654 2828

#182
Lane's Edge
Cuisines: Café, Bar, Mediterranean
Average Price: Modest
Area: Melbourne
Address: 39 Bourke St
Melbourne Victoria 3000
Phone: +61 3 9654 2409

#183
Collins Kitchen
Cuisines: Buffet
Average Price: Modest
Area: Melbourne
Address: 123 Collins St
Melbourne Victoria 3000
Phone: +61 3 9657 1234

#184
Rex Tremendae
Cuisines: Coffee, Tea, Café
Average Price: Inexpensive
Area: Melbourne
Address: 555 Flinders Ln
Melbourne Victoria 3000
Phone: +61 4 0183 7674

#185
Minh Xuong Seafood & BBQ Restaurant
Cuisines: Asian Fusion, Chinese
Average Price: Inexpensive
Area: Melbourne
Address: 209-211 Russell St
Melbourne Victoria 3000
Phone: +61 3 9663 2895

#186
European Bier Cafe
Cuisines: Pub, Music Venues, Gastropub
Average Price: Modest
Area: Melbourne
Address: 120 Exhibition St
Melbourne Victoria 3000
Phone: +61 3 9663 1222

#187
Gaylord
Cuisines: Indian, Vegetarian
Average Price: Modest
Area: Melbourne
Address: 4 Tattersalls Lane
Melbourne Victoria 3000
Phone: +61 3 9663 3980

#188
No 35
Cuisines: European
Average Price: Exclusive
Area: Melbourne
Address: 25 Collins St
Melbourne Victoria 3000
Phone: +61 3 9653 7744

#189
Crazy Wing
Cuisines: Chinese
Average Price: Inexpensive
Area: Melbourne
Address: 177 Russell St
Melbourne Victoria 3000
Phone: +61 3 9663 6555

#190
Nihonshu
Cuisines: Japanese, Lounge
Average Price: Modest
Area: Melbourne
Address: 163 Lonsdale St
Melbourne Victoria 3000
Phone: +61 3 9663 8118

#191
Don-Bay
Cuisines: Fast Food, Japanese
Average Price: Inexpensive
Area: Melbourne
Address: 440 Collins St
Melbourne Victoria 3000
Phone: +61 3 9670 3456

#192
Phò Nom
Cuisines: Vietnamese, Fast Food
Average Price: Inexpensive
Area: Melbourne
Address: 287 Lonsdale St
Melbourne Victoria 3000
Phone: +61 3 8609 8221

#193
Kim Sing
Cuisines: Vegetarian, Chinese
Average Price: Inexpensive
Area: Melbourne
Address: 232 Flinders St
Melbourne Victoria 3000
Phone: +61 3 9654 7889

#194
Squires Loft City Steakhouse
Cuisines: Steakhouse
Average Price: Expensive
Area: Melbourne
Address: 12 Goldie Pl
Melbourne Victoria 3000
Phone: +61 3 9670 7317

#195
Tazio Birraria And Pizzeria
Cuisines: Italian, Pizza
Average Price: Modest
Area: Melbourne
Address: 66 Flinders Lane
Melbourne Victoria 3000
Phone: +61 3 9654 9119

#196
Mail Exchange Hotel
Cuisines: Pub, Gastropub
Average Price: Modest
Area: Melbourne
Address: 688 Bourke St
Melbourne Victoria 3000
Phone: +61 3 9903 6880

#197
The Soup Place
Cuisines: Soup
Average Price: Inexpensive
Area: Melbourne
Address: 14 Centre Pl
Melbourne Victoria 3000
Phone: +61 4 1255 3449

#198
Longroom
Cuisines: Lounge, Cocktail Bar, Australian
Average Price: Modest
Area: Melbourne
Address: 162-168 Collins St
Melbourne Victoria 3000
Phone: +61 3 9663 7226

#199
The Mill
Cuisines: European
Average Price: Modest
Area: Melbourne
Address: 71 Hardware Lane
Melbourne Victoria 3000
Phone: +61 3 9600 1454

#200
Three Below
Cuisines: Bar, Tapas
Average Price: Modest
Area: Melbourne
Address: 3 City Sq
Melbourne Victoria 3006
Phone: +61 3 9662 9555

#201
Red Pepper
Cuisines: Indian
Average Price: Modest
Area: Melbourne
Address: 14 Bourke St
Melbourne Victoria 3000
Phone: +61 3 9654 5714

#202
Affogato
Cuisines: Café
Average Price: Modest
Area: Melbourne
Address: 29 Hardware
Melbourne Victoria 3000
Phone: +61 3 9642 5593

#203
Naked Espresso Bar
Cuisines: Coffee, Tea, Café
Average Price: Inexpensive
Area: Melbourne
Address: 390 Lt Bourke St
Melbourne Victoria 3000
Phone: +61 4 1177 3559

#204
Kalamaki
Cuisines: Greek
Average Price: Inexpensive
Area: Melbourne
Address: 389 Lonsdale St
Melbourne Victoria 3000
Phone: +61 3 9602 4444

#205
Thai Culinary
Cuisines: Thai
Average Price: Inexpensive
Area: Melbourne
Address: 433 Elizabeth St
Melbourne Victoria 3000
Phone: +61 3 9328 3812

#206
Rose Garden BBQ
Cuisines: Chinese
Average Price: Inexpensive
Area: Melbourne
Address: 435 Elizabeth St
Melbourne Victoria 3000
Phone: +61 3 9329 1560

#207
Cafe Andiamo
Cuisines: Café, European
Average Price: Modest
Area: Melbourne
Address: 36-38 Degraves St
Melbourne Victoria 3000
Phone: +61 3 9650 8060

#208
Il Tempo Bar Caffe Bruschetteria
Cuisines: Café, Italian
Average Price: Modest
Area: Melbourne
Address: 250 Flinders St
Melbourne Victoria 3000
Phone: +61 3 9663 7522

#209
The Last Jar
Cuisines: Irish, Gastropub
Average Price: Modest
Area: Melbourne
Address: 616 Elizabeth St
Melbourne Victoria 3000
Phone: +61 3 9348 2957

#210
State Of Grace
Cuisines: Cocktail Bar, Australian
Average Price: Expensive
Area: Melbourne
Address: 477 Collins St
Melbourne Victoria 3000
Phone: +61 3 8644 7110

#211
Quanjude
Cuisines: Chinese
Average Price: Expensive
Area: Melbourne
Address: 299 Queen St
Melbourne Victoria 3000
Phone: +61 3 9670 0091

#212
Byblos Bar & Restaurant
Cuisines: Mediterranean
Average Price: Modest
Area: Docklands
Address: 18-30 Siddeley St
Melbourne Victoria 3000
Phone: +61 3 9614 6400

#213
POP Restaurant
Cuisines: Australian
Average Price: Modest
Area: Melbourne
Address: 68 Hardware Ln
Melbourne Victoria 3000
Phone: +61 3 9642 1341

#214
Bluestone
Cuisines: Venues, Event Space, Australian
Average Price: Expensive
Area: Melbourne
Address: 349 Flinders Ln
Melbourne Victoria 3000
Phone: +61 3 9620 4060

#215
Hot Star Large Fried Chicken
Cuisines: Taiwanese
Average Price: Inexpensive
Area: Melbourne
Address: 233 Swanston St
Melbourne Victoria 3000
Phone: +61 4 8113 4291

#216
Perkup Burgers
Cuisines: Burgers
Average Price: Inexpensive
Area: Melbourne
Address: 12 Degraves St
Melbourne Victoria 3000
Phone: +61 3 9671 4069

Melbourne Restaurant Guide / Restaurants, Bars & Cafés

#217
Pastuso
Cuisines: Latin American, Peruvian
Average Price: Expensive
Area: Melbourne
Address: 19 Acdc Lane
Melbourne Victoria 3000
Phone: +61 3 9662 4556

#218
Perkup
Cuisines: Café
Average Price: Modest
Area: Melbourne
Address: 610 Collins St
Melbourne Victoria 3000
Phone: +61 3 9620 2837

#219
TGI Fridays Melbourne Central
Cuisines: American
Average Price: Expensive
Area: Melbourne
Address: Cnr La Trobe & Swanston St
Melbourne Victoria 3000
Phone: +61 3 9650 3322

#220
The Fair Trader
Cuisines: Café, Breakfast & Brunch, Sandwiches
Average Price: Modest
Area: Melbourne
Address: 11 Exhibition St
Melbourne Victoria 3000
Phone: +61 3 9078 7544

#221
Il Bacaro
Cuisines: Italian
Average Price: Expensive
Area: Melbourne
Address: 168-170 Little Collins St
Melbourne Victoria 3000
Phone: +61 3 9654 6778

#222
The Trust
Cuisines: European
Average Price: Modest
Area: Melbourne
Address: 405 Flinders Ln
Melbourne Victoria 3000
Phone: +61 3 9629 9300

#223
Sally's Kitchen
Cuisines: Café
Average Price: Modest
Area: Melbourne
Address: 295 Exhibition St
Melbourne Victoria 3000
Phone: +61 3 9650 9222

#224
Von Haus
Cuisines: Café, Wine Bar
Average Price: Modest
Area: Melbourne
Address: 1 Crossley St
Melbourne Victoria 3000
Phone: +61 3 9662 2756

#225
STREAT
Cuisines: Café, Coffee, Tea
Average Price: Inexpensive
Area: Melbourne
Address: 5 Mckillop St
Melbourne Victoria 3000
Phone: +61 3 9629 4222

#226
Izakaya Sushi Bar
Cuisines: Japanese
Average Price: Inexpensive
Area: Melbourne
Address: 211 La Trobe St
Melbourne Victoria 3000
Phone: +61 3 9639 3559

#227
Decoy Cafe
Cuisines: Café
Average Price: Modest
Area: Melbourne
Address: 303 Exhibition St
Melbourne Victoria 3000
Phone: +61 3 9650 6077

#228
Vapiano
Cuisines: Italian
Average Price: Modest
Area: Melbourne
Address: Flinders Lane
Melbourne Victoria 3000
Phone: +61 3 9620 3335

Melbourne Restaurant Guide / Restaurants, Bars & Cafés

#229
Gekkazan
Cuisines: Japanese, Sushi Bar
Average Price: Modest
Area: Melbourne
Address: 350 Bourke St
Melbourne Victoria 3000
Phone: +44 39 963 7767

#230
The Pancake Parlour
Cuisines: Crêperie, Desserts, Breakfast & Brunch
Average Price: Modest
Area: Melbourne
Address: 211 La Trobe St
Melbourne Victoria 3000
Phone: +61 3 9654 3177

#231
Pho24
Cuisines: Vietnamese
Average Price: Inexpensive
Area: Melbourne
Address: 656 Little Bourke St
Melbourne Victoria 3000
Phone: +61 3 5915 9047

#232
Soul Kitchen Woodfired Pizza
Cuisines: Food Truck, Pizza
Average Price: Inexpensive
Area: Southbank, Melbourne
Address: 80 St Kilda Rd
Melbourne Victoria 3004
Phone: +61 4 0854 4899

#233
Grill Room Steakhouse City
Cuisines: Restaurant
Average Price: Expensive
Area: Melbourne
Address: 535 Little Lonsdale St
Melbourne Victoria 3000
Phone: +61 3 9602 2228

#234
Kum Den Chinese Restaurant
Cuisines: Restaurant
Average Price: Modest
Area: Melbourne
Address: 3-5 Waratah Pl
Melbourne Victoria 3000
Phone: +61 3 9663 6508

#235
RMB Cafe
Cuisines: Café, Breakfast & Brunch
Average Price: Modest
Area: Melbourne
Address: 37 Degraves St
Melbourne Victoria 3000
Phone: +61 3 9671 4455

#236
Oporto
Cuisines: Fast Food, Burgers
Average Price: Inexpensive
Area: Melbourne
Address: Level 2 240 Lonsdale St
Melbourne Victoria 3000
Phone: +61 3 9654 6366

#237
Cafenatics On Equitable Place
Cuisines: Café
Average Price: Modest
Area: Melbourne
Address: 330 Collins St
Melbourne Victoria 3000
Phone: +61 3 9642 4000

#238
Hairy Little Sista
Cuisines: Bar, African, Spanish
Average Price: Modest
Area: Melbourne
Address: 230 Little Collins St
Melbourne Victoria 3000
Phone: +61 3 9639 7778

#239
Sushi Sushi
Cuisines: Fast Food, Sushi Bar, Japanese
Average Price: Inexpensive
Area: Melbourne
Address: Ground Level, Shop OK12, Melbourne Central, 300 Lonsdale St
Melbourne Victoria 3000
Phone: +61 3 9639 0065

#240
Burma Lane
Cuisines: Burmese, Tapas
Average Price: Modest
Area: Melbourne
Address: 118 Little Collins St
Melbourne Victoria 3000
Phone: +61 3 9615 8500

Melbourne Restaurant Guide / Restaurants, Bars & Cafés

#241
Sarti
Cuisines: Wine Bar, Italian
Average Price: Expensive
Area: Melbourne
Address: 6 Russell Pl
Melbourne Victoria 3000
Phone: +61 3 9636 7822

#242
Ramen Ya
Cuisines: Japanese
Average Price: Inexpensive
Area: Melbourne
Address: Shop 9, 108 Bourke St
Melbourne Victoria 3000
Phone: +61 3 9662 1001

#243
Ramen Ya
Cuisines: Japanese
Average Price: Inexpensive
Area: Melbourne
Address: 350 Bourke St
Melbourne Victoria 3000
Phone: +61 3 9654 5838

#244
Wagamama
Cuisines: Asian Fusion
Average Price: Expensive
Area: Melbourne
Address: 83 Flinders La
Melbourne Victoria 3000
Phone: +61 3 9671 4303

#245
Sushi Ten
Cuisines: Sushi Bar, Japanese
Average Price: Inexpensive
Area: Melbourne
Address: Shop 14-15, Port Phillip Arc,
228 Flinders St Melbourne Victoria 3000
Phone: +61 3 9639 6296

#246
Simpsons Chips & Burgers
Cuisines: Fast Food
Average Price: Modest
Area: Melbourne
Address: 143 Russell St
Melbourne Victoria 3000
Phone: +61 3 9041 6602

#247
Tjanabi Restaurant
Cuisines: Restaurant
Average Price: Expensive
Area: Melbourne
Address: 2 Flinders St
Melbourne Victoria 3000
Phone: +61 3 9662 1225

#248
Lord Of The Fries
Cuisines: Burgers, Vegan, Fast Food
Average Price: Inexpensive
Area: Melbourne
Address: 211 La Trobe St
Melbourne Victoria 3000
Phone: +61 9 5213 227

#249
El Sabor
Cuisines: Mexican
Average Price: Modest
Area: North Melbourne
Address: 500 Victoria St
Melbourne Victoria 3051
Phone: +61 3 9329 9477

#250
Lounge
Cuisines: Lounge, Café
Average Price: Modest
Area: Melbourne
Address: 243 Swanston St
Melbourne Victoria 3000
Phone: +61 3 9663 2916

#251
Laurent
Cuisines: Bakery, Café
Average Price: Modest
Area: Melbourne
Address: 306 Little Collins St
Melbourne Victoria 3000
Phone: +61 3 9654 1011

#252
Brown Alley
Cuisines: Dance Club, Pub Food
Average Price: Modest
Area: Melbourne
Address: Cnr Lonsdale St & King St
Melbourne Victoria 3000
Phone: +61 9 6708 599

#253
Arintji
Cuisines: Venues, Event Space, Tapas, Café
Average Price: Modest
Area: Melbourne
Address: Federation Square Shop 26/ 2 Swanston St Melbourne Victoria 3000
Phone: +61 3 9663 9900

#254
Sheni's Curries
Cuisines: Fast Food, Indian
Average Price: Inexpensive
Area: Melbourne
Address: 161 Collins St Melbourne Victoria 3000
Phone: +61 3 9654 3535

#255
Rare Steakhouse
Cuisines: Steakhouse
Average Price: Expensive
Area: Melbourne
Address: 61 Little Collins St Melbourne Victoria 3000
Phone: +61 3 9663 3373

#256
Eleven Inch Pizzeria
Cuisines: Pizza, Italian
Average Price: Inexpensive
Area: Melbourne
Address: 353-359 Little Collins St Melbourne Victoria 3000
Phone: +61 3 9602 5333

#257
Mr Huang Jin
Cuisines: Taiwanese
Average Price: Modest
Area: Melbourne
Address: 525 Collins St Melbourne Victoria 3000
Phone: +61 3 9077 7937

#258
Menya Ramen
Cuisines: Sushi Bar, Japanese
Average Price: Inexpensive
Area: Melbourne
Address: 210 La Trobe St Melbourne Victoria 3000
Phone: +61 3 9639 3383

#259
Shanghai Noodle House
Cuisines: Shanghainese
Average Price: Inexpensive
Area: Melbourne
Address: 15 Tattersalls Ln Melbourne Victoria 3000
Phone: +61 3 9662 9380

#260
The Organic Food & Wine Deli
Cuisines: Vegan, Gluten-Free, Deli
Average Price: Inexpensive
Area: Melbourne
Address: 28 Degraves St Melbourne Victoria 3000
Phone: +61 3 9654 5157

#261
Paperboy Kitchen
Cuisines: Fast Food, Asian Fusion
Average Price: Inexpensive
Area: Melbourne
Address: 320 Little Lonsdale St Melbourne Victoria 3000
Phone: +61 3 9642 0147

#262
The Workers' Food Room
Cuisines: Café, Gluten-Free
Average Price: Modest
Area: Melbourne
Address: 472 Little Lonsdale St Melbourne Victoria 3000
Phone: +61 3 9602 3220

#263
Sakae Japanese Cafe
Cuisines: Japanese
Average Price: Inexpensive
Area: Melbourne
Address: Shop 1/280 King St Melbourne Victoria 3000
Phone: +61 3 9642 1635

#264
Pancake Dessert House
Cuisines: Chinese
Average Price: Inexpensive
Area: Melbourne
Address: Shop 18 200 Bourke St Melbourne Victoria 3000
Phone: +61 3 9663 1400

#265
Zhen Hong
Cuisines: Cantonese
Average Price: Modest
Area: Melbourne
Address: 191 Russell St
Melbourne Victoria 3000
Phone: +61 3 9650 8815

#266
Golden Monkey
Cuisines: Dim Sum, Lounge
Average Price: Exclusive
Area: Melbourne
Address: 389 Lonsdale St
Melbourne Victoria 3000
Phone: +61 3 9602 2055

#267
Be-Hive Cafe Bar
Cuisines: Café
Average Price: Inexpensive
Area: Melbourne
Address: 459 Collins St
Melbourne Victoria 3000
Phone: +61 3 9614 0019

#268
The Kitchen Royale
Cuisines: Turkish, Ethnic Food
Average Price: Inexpensive
Area: Melbourne
Address: Royal Arcade, 335 Bourke St
Melbourne Victoria 3000
Phone: +61 4 0162 7304

#269
The Press Club
Cuisines: Greek
Average Price: Exclusive
Area: Melbourne
Address: 72 Flinders St
Melbourne Victoria 3000
Phone: +61 3 9677 9677

#270
Vietnam Noodle House
Cuisines: Vietnamese
Average Price: Inexpensive
Area: Melbourne
Address: 251 Swanston St
Melbourne Victoria 3000
Phone: +61 3 9639 4911

#271
Delicious Delight Cafe
Cuisines: Café
Average Price: Inexpensive
Area: Melbourne
Address: 113 Swanston St
Melbourne Victoria 3000
Phone: +61 3 9662 3347

#272
Pacific BBQ Cafe
Cuisines: Chinese, Seafood
Average Price: Modest
Area: Melbourne
Address: 213 Lonsdale St
Melbourne Victoria 3000
Phone: +61 3 9663 9288

#273
Chick-In
Cuisines: Korean
Average Price: Inexpensive
Area: Melbourne
Address: G23, 620 Collins St
Melbourne Victoria 3000
Phone: +61 3 9973 6244

#274
Corner And Bench
Cuisines: Café
Average Price: Inexpensive
Area: Melbourne
Address: 408 Bourke St
Melbourne Victoria 3000
Phone: +61 3 9602 4777

#275
Sensory Lab
Cuisines: Café, Coffee, Tea
Average Price: Inexpensive
Area: Melbourne
Address: 297 Little Collins St
Melbourne Victoria 3000
Phone: +61 3 9645 0065

#276
Timeout Cafe
Cuisines: Café, Mediterranean, Breakfast & Brunch
Average Price: Exclusive
Area: Melbourne
Address: 2 Swanston St
Melbourne Victoria 3000
Phone: +61 3 9671 3855

#277
Brunetti
Cuisines: Café, Bakery, Italian
Average Price: Inexpensive
Area: Melbourne
Address: 214 Flinders Ln
Melbourne Victoria 3000
Phone: +61 3 9663 8085

#278
Sezar
Cuisines: Tapas, Middle Eastern
Average Price: Expensive
Area: Melbourne
Address: 6 Melbourne Pl
Melbourne Victoria 3000
Phone: +61 3 9663 9882

#279
Killiney Kopitiam
Cuisines: Singaporean, Malaysian
Average Price: Modest
Area: Melbourne
Address: 108 Bourke St
Melbourne Victoria 3000
Phone: +61 3 9663 5818

#280
Mad Mex
Cuisines: Mexican
Average Price: Inexpensive
Area: Melbourne
Address: Shop 35, 5 Elizabeth St
Melbourne Victoria 3000
Phone: +61 3 9620 2367

#281
Etto
Cuisines: Italian, Fast Food
Average Price: Inexpensive
Area: Melbourne
Address: 261 Clarendon St
Melbourne Victoria 3205
Phone: +61 3 9696 3886

#282
Society
Cuisines: Italian, Lounge
Average Price: Modest
Area: Melbourne
Address: 23 Bourke St
Melbourne Victoria 3000
Phone: +61 3 9639 2544

#283
Bambini Barrista
Cuisines: Café, Coffee, Tea
Average Price: Inexpensive
Area: Melbourne
Address: 530 Little Collins St
Melbourne Victoria 3000
Phone: +61 3 9614 0023

#284
The Mess Hall
Cuisines: Italian, Breakfast & Brunch
Average Price: Modest
Area: Melbourne
Address: 51 Bourke St
Melbourne Victoria 3000
Phone: +61 3 9654 6800

#285
Boney
Cuisines: Asian Fusion, Music Venues
Average Price: Modest
Area: Melbourne
Address: 68 Little Collins St
Melbourne Victoria 3000
Phone: +61 3 9663 8268

#286
Green Pepper
Cuisines: Indian
Average Price: Modest
Area: Melbourne
Address: 18 Bourke St
Melbourne Victoria 3000
Phone: +61 3 9662 2963

#287
The Elephant & Wheelbarrow
Cuisines: Pub, British
Average Price: Modest
Area: Melbourne
Address: 96 Bourke St
Melbourne Victoria 3000
Phone: +61 3 9639 8444

#288
Witches In Britches Theatre Restaurant
Cuisines: Restaurant
Average Price: Exclusive
Area: West Melbourne
Address: 84 Dudley St
Melbourne Victoria 3003
Phone: +61 3 9329 9850

Melbourne Restaurant Guide / Restaurants, Bars & Cafés

#289
Claypots Evening Star
Cuisines: Seafood
Average Price: Modest
Area: Melbourne
Address: South
Melbourne Market
Melbourne Victoria 3205
Phone: +61 3 9645 5779

#290
Sea Salt Fish & Sushi Bar
Cuisines: Fast Food, Fish & Chips
Average Price: Inexpensive
Area: Melbourne
Address: 13 Degraves St
Melbourne Victoria 3000
Phone: +61 3 9654 2095

#291
Fo Guang Yuan Art Gallery
Cuisines: Art Gallery, Tea Room, Vegetarian
Average Price: Inexpensive
Area: Melbourne
Address: 141 Queen St
Melbourne Victoria 3000
Phone: +61 3 9642 2388

#292
Menya
Cuisines: Japanese
Average Price: Inexpensive
Area: Melbourne
Address: 437 Elizabeth St
Melbourne Victoria 3000
Phone: +61 3 9328 8928

#293
Orient East
Cuisines: Malaysian, Bar
Average Price: Modest
Area: Melbourne
Address: 348 St Kilda Rd
Melbourne Victoria 3004
Phone: +61 3 9685 2900

#294
Saint & Rogue
Cuisines: Pub, Australian
Average Price: Modest
Area: Melbourne
Address: 582 Little Collins St
Melbourne Victoria 3000
Phone: +61 3 9620 9720

#295
Swanston Walk Cafe Bar
Cuisines: Café, Pizza, Italian
Average Price: Inexpensive
Area: Melbourne
Address: 157 Swanston St
Melbourne Victoria 3000
Phone: +61 3 9654 0990

#296
11 Inch Pizza
Cuisines: Pizza
Average Price: Modest
Area: Melbourne
Address: 353-359 Lt Collins St
Melbourne Victoria
Phone: +61 9 6025 333

#297
Ajisen Ramen
Cuisines: Japanese
Average Price: Inexpensive
Area: Melbourne
Address: 211 La Trobe St
Melbourne Victoria 3000
Phone: +61 3 9650 8986

#298
Ba'get - Russell St
Cuisines: Vietnamese, Bakery
Average Price: Inexpensive
Area: Melbourne
Address: 132 Russel St
Melbourne Victoria 3000
Phone: +61 4 9012 1199

#299
Funky Curry
Cuisines: Fast Food, Indian
Average Price: Inexpensive
Area: Melbourne
Address: 164 Bourke St
Melbourne Victoria 3000
Phone: +61 3 9662 2299

#300
Little Cupcakes
Cuisines: Desserts, Café, Bakery
Average Price: Inexpensive
Area: Melbourne
Address: 7 Degraves St
Melbourne Victoria 3000
Phone: +61 3 9077 0413

#301
White Tomato
Cuisines: Korean
Average Price: Modest
Area: Melbourne
Address: 160 - 162 Bourke St
Melbourne Victoria 3000
Phone: +61 3 9663 0370

#302
Dumpling Sisters
Cuisines: Chinese
Average Price: Inexpensive
Area: Melbourne
Address: 229 Exhibition St
Melbourne Victoria 3000
Phone: +61 3 9663 1888

#303
International Diethnes Cakes
Cuisines: Bakery, Fast Food, Desserts
Average Price: Modest
Area: Melbourne
Address: 185 Lonsdale St
Melbourne Victoria 3000
Phone: +61 3 9663 2092

#304
Harajuku Crepes
Cuisines: Desserts, Crêperie
Average Price: Inexpensive
Area: Melbourne
Address: Shp148 316 Elizabeth St
Melbourne Victoria 3000
Phone: +61 3 9654 9775

#305
Blanc Cafe Bar
Cuisines: Café
Average Price: Inexpensive
Area: Melbourne
Address: 140 King St
Melbourne Victoria 3000
Phone: +61 3 9620 3222

#306
Monkey Bar
Cuisines: Fast Food
Average Price: Inexpensive
Area: Melbourne
Address: 10 King St
Melbourne Victoria 3000
Phone: +61 3 9614 5354

#307
Cafenatics
Cuisines: Australian, Coffee, Tea
Average Price: Inexpensive
Area: Melbourne
Address: 500 Collins St
Melbourne Victoria 3000
Phone: +61 3 9629 4440

#308
Petty Session Cafe
Cuisines: Café
Average Price: Inexpensive
Area: Melbourne
Address: 255 William St
Melbourne Victoria 3000
Phone: +61 3 9600 0311

#309
City BBQ Chinese Restaurant
Cuisines: Chinese
Average Price: Modest
Area: Melbourne
Address: 178 Little Bourke St
Melbourne Victoria 3000
Phone: +61 3 9663 2311

#310
Swiss Club Restaurant
Cuisines: Fondue, French, German
Average Price: Modest
Area: Melbourne
Address: 89 Flinders Ln
Melbourne Victoria 3000
Phone: +61 3 9650 1196

#311
Money Order Office
MOO Restaurant & Wine Bar
Cuisines: Restaurant
Average Price: Expensive
Area: Melbourne
Address: 318 Little Bourke St
Melbourne Victoria 3000
Phone: +61 3 9639 3020

#312
Slate Restaurant And Bar
Cuisines: Bar, Australian,
Venues, Event Space
Average Price: Modest
Area: Melbourne
Address: 9 Goldsbrough Ln
Melbourne Victoria 3000
Phone: +61 3 9670 4311

Melbourne Restaurant Guide / Restaurants, Bars & Cafés

#313
Brother Thomas
Cuisines: Coffee, Tea, Restaurant
Average Price: Modest
Area: Melbourne
Address: 350 William St
Melbourne Victoria 3000
Phone: +61 3 9328 7535

#314
Roll'd
Cuisines: Vietnamese
Average Price: Inexpensive
Area: Melbourne
Address: 357 Collins St
Melbourne Victoria 3000
Phone: +61 3 9621 2227

#315
Langleys Cafe
Cuisines: Café
Average Price: Inexpensive
Area: Melbourne
Address: 670 Bourke St
Melbourne Victoria 3000
Phone: +61 3 9642 2822

#316
Pomodoro Sardo Taste Of Sardinia
Cuisines: Pizza, Italian
Average Price: Modest
Area: Melbourne
Address: 118 Lonsdale St
Melbourne Victoria 3000
Phone: +61 3 9663 8006

#317
Mezzo Bar & Grill
Cuisines: Wine Bar, Italian
Average Price: Expensive
Area: Melbourne
Address: 35 Little Bourke St
Melbourne Victoria 3000
Phone: +61 3 9650 0988

#318
Lupino Italian Bistro
Cuisines: Italian
Average Price: Expensive
Area: Melbourne
Address: 41 Little Collins St
Melbourne Victoria 3000
Phone: +61 3 9639 0333

#319
Shanghai Dynasty Restaurant
Cuisines: Restaurant
Average Price: Expensive
Area: Melbourne
Address: 206 Bourke St
Melbourne Victoria 3000
Phone: +61 3 9663 7770

#320
Dessert Story
Cuisines: Desserts, Chinese
Average Price: Inexpensive
Area: Melbourne
Address: 305 Swanston St
Melbourne Victoria 3000
Phone: +61 3 9663 8862

#321
Stellini Bar
Cuisines: Café, Bar, Italian
Average Price: Modest
Area: Melbourne
Address: 198 Little Collins St
Melbourne Victoria 3000
Phone: +61 3 9654 5074

#322
Maitai
Cuisines: Thai, Bar
Average Price: Modest
Area: Melbourne
Address: 234A Russell St
Melbourne Victoria 3000
Phone: +61 3 9663 2112

#323
Yuzu Cafe And Cuisine
Cuisines: Japanese, Café
Average Price: Modest
Area: Melbourne
Address: Rear 480 Collins St
Melbourne Victoria 3000
Phone: +61 3 9620 1177

#324
Waffle On
Cuisines: Desserts, Coffee, Sandwiches
Average Price: Inexpensive
Area: Melbourne
Address: 9 Degraves St
Melbourne Victoria 3000
Phone: +61 4 0140 8168

#325
Dose Espresso
Cuisines: Café
Average Price: Inexpensive
Area: Melbourne
Address: 155 Queen St
Melbourne Victoria 3000
Phone: +61 3 9602 4067

#326
Tokyo Maki
Cuisines: Japanese
Average Price: Modest
Area: Melbourne
Address: Shop 5 / 547 Flinders St
Melbourne Victoria 3000
Phone: +61 3 9620 0375

#327
Flora
Cuisines: Indian
Average Price: Modest
Area: Melbourne
Address: Shp 2/ 238 A Flinders St
Melbourne Victoria 3000
Phone: +61 3 9663 1212

#328
Rim Thang
Cuisines: Thai
Average Price: Inexpensive
Area: Melbourne
Address: 417-419 Elizabeth St
Melbourne Victoria 3000
Phone: +61 3 9328 3820

#329
LB2
Cuisines: Café
Average Price: Inexpensive
Area: Melbourne
Address: 2 Gallagher Pl
Melbourne Victoria 3000
Phone: +61 4 1701 3958

#330
Yoyogi
Cuisines: Restaurant
Average Price: Inexpensive
Area: Melbourne
Address: 213 Swanston St
Melbourne Victoria 3000
Phone: +61 3 9663 7266

#331
Blue Fish
Cuisines: Fish & Chips
Average Price: Inexpensive
Area: Melbourne
Address: 16 Centre Place
Melbourne Victoria 3000
Phone: +61 9 6630 738

#332
Mr Big Stuff
Cuisines: American
Average Price: Expensive
Area: Melbourne
Address: 15 Meyers Pl
Melbourne Victoria 3000
Phone: +61 3 9639 7411

#333
Two Fingers
Cuisines: Café
Average Price: Modest
Area: Melbourne
Address: 27 Russell St
Melbourne Victoria 3000
Phone: +61 3 9663 0202

#334
Stokehouse City
Cuisines: Venues, Event Space, Australian, Steakhouse
Average Price: Modest
Area: Melbourne
Address: 7 Alfred Pl
Melbourne Victoria 3000
Phone: +61 3 9525 5555

#335
Mad Mex
Cuisines: Mexican
Average Price: Modest
Area: Melbourne
Address: 121 Exhibition St
Melbourne Victoria 3000
Phone: +61 3 9650 1122

#336
Bluebag
Cuisines: Coffee, Tea, Sandwiches
Average Price: Inexpensive
Area: Melbourne
Address: 84 Exhibition St
Melbourne Victoria 3000
Phone: +61 3 9639 3125

Melbourne Restaurant Guide / Restaurants, Bars & Cafés

#337
Basement Espresso Cafe & Meeting Space
Cuisines: Café
Average Price: Inexpensive
Area: Melbourne
Address: 31 Niagara Ln
Melbourne Victoria 3000
Phone: +61 3 9624 8700

#338
Nourish Salads
Cuisines: Salad
Average Price: Inexpensive
Area: Melbourne
Address: 3/221 Queen St
Melbourne Victoria 3000
Phone: +61 3 9642 2556

#339
Nando's
Cuisines: Portuguese, Fast Food
Average Price: Inexpensive
Area: Melbourne
Address: 168 Bourke St
Melbourne Victoria 3000
Phone: +61 3 9654 4572

#340
Monga Sweet Cafe
Cuisines: Café
Average Price: Inexpensive
Area: Melbourne
Address: 217 Russell St
Melbourne Victoria 3000
Phone: +61 3 9654 4885

#341
Feddish
Cuisines: Gastropub, Australian
Average Price: Expensive
Area: Melbourne
Address: Federation Sq
Melbourne Victoria 3000
Phone: +61 3 9654 5855

#342
School Of Life
Cuisines: Adult Education, Café, Bookstore
Average Price: Inexpensive
Area: Melbourne
Address: 669 Little Bourke St
Melbourne Victoria 3000
Phone: +61 3 9077 8724

#343
Pepperoni's
Cuisines: Italian, Pizza
Average Price: Expensive
Area: Melbourne
Address: 7a Elizabeth St
Melbourne Victoria 3000
Phone: +61 3 9614 2274

#344
Crisp Salad Bar
Cuisines: Health Market, Salad, Fast Food
Average Price: Inexpensive
Area: Melbourne
Address: Shop TG20 Goldsbrough Ln
Melbourne Victoria 3000
Phone: +61 4 3955 9829

#345
Benito's
Cuisines: Italian, Bar
Average Price: Modest
Area: Melbourne
Address: 445 Little Collins St
Melbourne Victoria 3000
Phone: +61 3 9670 5347

#346
Colonial Hotel
Cuisines: Mediterranean, Parma, Australian
Average Price: Modest
Area: Melbourne
Address: 585 Lonsdale St
Melbourne Victoria 3000
Phone: +61 3 9670 8599

#347
Suri Suri
Cuisines: Japanese, Korean
Average Price: Inexpensive
Area: Melbourne
Address: 601 Little Collins St
Melbourne Victoria 3000
Phone: +61 3 9629 9797

#348
Dion Greek & Seafood Restaurant
Cuisines: Greek
Average Price: Expensive
Area: Melbourne
Address: 207 Lonsdale St
Melbourne Victoria 3000
Phone: +61 3 9650 4050

#349
Self Preservation
Cuisines: Coffee, Tea, Italian
Average Price: Modest
Area: Melbourne
Address: 70 Bourke St
Melbourne Victoria 3000
Phone: +61 3 9650 0523

#350
Claypot King
Cuisines: Chinese
Average Price: Modest
Area: Melbourne
Address: 209 Swanston St
Melbourne Victoria 3000
Phone: +61 3 9662 3222

#351
THR1VE
Cuisines: Health Market, Gluten-Free, Fast Food
Average Price: Modest
Area: Melbourne
Address: 287 Lonsdale St
Melbourne Victoria 3000
Phone: +61 3 8609 8221

#352
Mr Tulk
Cuisines: Coffee, Tea, Breakfast & Brunch
Average Price: Modest
Area: Melbourne
Address: 328 Swanston St
Melbourne Victoria 3000
Phone: +61 3 8660 5700

#353
Lucy Liu
Cuisines: Asian Fusion
Average Price: Expensive
Area: Melbourne
Address: 23 Oliver Lane
Melbourne Victoria 3000
Phone: +61 3 9639 5777

#354
Spices Connection
Cuisines: Food Court, Szechuan, Thai
Average Price: Inexpensive
Area: Melbourne
Address: Shop 14, Lower Ground Floor Food Court Melbourne Victoria
Phone: +61 3 9639 6688

#355
Ambrosia Protein
Cuisines: Café, Health Market
Average Price: Modest
Area: Melbourne
Address: 300 Flinders St
Melbourne Victoria 8000
Phone: +61 3 9620 4392

#356
Cafe Segovia
Cuisines: Café, Mediterranean
Average Price: Modest
Area: Melbourne
Address: 33 Block Pl
Melbourne Victoria 3000
Phone: +61 3 9650 2373

#357
Panzerotti
Cuisines: Italian, Fast Food
Average Price: Inexpensive
Area: Melbourne
Address: 289 Flinders Lane
Melbourne Victoria 3000
Phone: +61 3 9662 3321

#358
Tobu Sushi
Cuisines: Japanese, Sushi Bar
Average Price: Inexpensive
Area: Melbourne
Address: 45 Swanston St
Melbourne Victoria 3000
Phone: +61 3 9654 9996

#359
Melbourne Public
Cuisines: Bar, Gastropub
Average Price: Modest
Area: South Wharf
Address: 20 Convention Centre Pl
Melbourne Victoria 3006
Phone: +61 3 9268 7600

#360
Oriental Tea House
Cuisines: Dim Sum, Coffee, Tea
Average Price: Modest
Area: Melbourne
Address: 378 Little Collins St
Melbourne Victoria 3000
Phone: +61 3 9600 4230

Melbourne Restaurant Guide / Restaurants, Bars & Cafés

#361
Il Pom Italian
Cuisines: Italian
Average Price: Modest
Area: Carlton, Melbourne
Address: 2 Swanston St
Melbourne Victoria 3000
Phone: +61 3 9662 2282

#362
Mcdonald's
Cuisines: Burgers, Fast Food
Average Price: Inexpensive
Area: Melbourne
Address: 501-503 Elizabeth St
Melbourne Victoria 3000
Phone: +61 3 9326 8158

#363
Sud
Cuisines: Restaurant
Average Price: Modest
Area: Melbourne
Address: 219 King St
Melbourne Victoria 3000
Phone: +61 3 9670 8451

#364
Alice Thai
Cuisines: Thai
Average Price: Modest
Area: Melbourne
Address: 215 Little Collins St
Melbourne Victoria 3000
Phone: +61 3 9669 0026

#365
Ten Ren's Tea Station
Cuisines: Asian Fusion, Juice Bar, Bubble Tea
Average Price: Inexpensive
Area: Melbourne
Address: 146 Swanston St
Melbourne Victoria 3000
Phone: +61 3 9654 3268

#366
Brown Bagels
Cuisines: Café, Breakfast & Brunch
Average Price: Inexpensive
Area: Melbourne
Address: 353 Little Collins St
Melbourne Victoria 3000
Phone: +61 3 9670 9114

#367
Cafe Alcaston
Cuisines: Restaurant
Average Price: Modest
Area: Melbourne
Address: 2 Collins St
Melbourne Victoria 3000
Phone: +61 3 9650 9387

#368
Laksa Me
Cuisines: Asian Fusion, Malaysian, Thai
Average Price: Modest
Area: Melbourne
Address: 1/16 Liverpool St
Melbourne Victoria 3000
Phone: +61 3 9639 9885

#369
Oishii Sushi
Cuisines: Fast Food, Sushi Bar
Average Price: Inexpensive
Area: Melbourne
Address: 236 Bourke St
Melbourne Victoria 3000
Phone: +61 3 9663 7793

#370
The Order Of Melbourne
Cuisines: Bar, Gastropub, Venues, Event Space
Average Price: Modest
Area: Melbourne
Address: 401 Swanston St
Melbourne Victoria 3000
Phone: +61 3 9663 6707

#371
Egg Sake Bistro
Cuisines: Japanese, Asian Fusion
Average Price: Inexpensive
Area: Parkville
Address: University Of Melbourne
Melbourne Victoria 3052
Phone: +61 3 9347 4704

#372
Dognation Russell
Cuisines: American, Coffee, Tea, Hot Dogs
Average Price: Inexpensive
Area: Melbourne
Address: 114 Russell St
Melbourne Victoria 3000
Phone: +61 3 9663 0078

#373
Five66
Cuisines: Café, Coffee, Tea, Breakfast & Brunch
Average Price: Inexpensive
Area: Melbourne
Address: 566 Flinders St
Melbourne Victoria 3000
Phone: +61 3 9614 0566

#374
Ants Bistro
Cuisines: Restaurant
Average Price: Expensive
Area: Melbourne
Address: 7 Corrs La
Melbourne Victoria 3000
Phone: +61 3 9639 2908

#375
Crêperie Le Triskel
Cuisines: Desserts, Crêperie, French
Average Price: Inexpensive
Area: Melbourne
Address: 32 Hardware Lane
Melbourne Victoria 3000
Phone: +61 4 6640 6404

#376
Piccolocino
Cuisines: Café, Coffee, Tea
Average Price: Inexpensive
Area: Melbourne
Address: Shp 8/ 540 Little Collins St
Melbourne Victoria 3000
Phone: +61 3 9629 5345

#377
Jardin Tan
Cuisines: Coffee, Tea, French, Vietnamese
Average Price: Modest
Area: Melbourne
Address: 100 Birdwood Ave
Melbourne Victoria 3004
Phone: +61 3 9691 3888

#378
Becco
Cuisines: Italian
Average Price: Expensive
Area: Melbourne
Address: 25 Crossley St
Melbourne Victoria 3000
Phone: +61 3 9663 3000

#379
Degraves Espresso Bar
Cuisines: Café, European, Vegetarian
Average Price: Modest
Area: Melbourne
Address: 23-25 Degraves St
Melbourne Victoria 3000
Phone: +61 3 9654 1245

#380
Regency Chinese Cuisine
Cuisines: Chinese
Average Price: Expensive
Area: Melbourne
Address: 232 King St
Melbourne Victoria 3000
Phone: +61 3 9600 3620

#381
Brothl
Cuisines: Soup, Coffee, Tea
Average Price: Modest
Area: Melbourne
Address: 123 Hardware St
Melbourne Victoria 3000
Phone: +61 3 9600 0588

#382
Dae Jang Geum Korean BBQ
Cuisines: Korean
Average Price: Inexpensive
Area: Melbourne
Address: 235 Little Bourke St
Melbourne Victoria 3000
Phone: +61 3 9662 9445

#383
Negroni's
Cuisines: Italian
Average Price: Modest
Area: Melbourne
Address: 477 Collins St
Melbourne Victoria 3000
Phone: +61 3 9614 1319

#384
Caboose Canteen
Cuisines: Café
Average Price: Modest
Area: Melbourne
Address: 4 City Sq
Melbourne Victoria 3000
Phone: +61 3 9663 4448

Melbourne Restaurant Guide / Restaurants, Bars & Cafés

#385
Yum Cha Cafe
Cuisines: Café, Dim Sum
Average Price: Modest
Area: Melbourne
Address: 193-195 Exhibition St
Melbourne Victoria 3000
Phone: +61 3 9662 9668

#386
Project 219
Cuisines: Breakfast & Brunch, Burgers
Average Price: Inexpensive
Area: Melbourne
Address: 219 Russell St
Melbourne Victoria 3000
Phone: +61 3 9663 1717

#387
Blahnik
Cuisines: Café, Italian
Average Price: Inexpensive
Area: Melbourne
Address: Shop B08, 385 Bourke St
Melbourne Victoria 3000
Phone: +61 3 9642 2234

#388
Momo
Cuisines: Middle Eastern, Mediterranean
Average Price: Exclusive
Area: Melbourne
Address: 123 Collins St
Melbourne Victoria 3000
Phone: +61 3 9650 0660

#389
Grill Steak Seafood
Cuisines: Seafood, Steakhouse
Average Price: Expensive
Area: Melbourne
Address: 66 Hardware Ln
Melbourne Victoria 3000
Phone: +61 3 9642 0776

#390
Starbucks
Cuisines: Café, Coffee, Tea
Average Price: Modest
Area: Melbourne
Address: 247 Bourke St
Melbourne Victoria 3000
Phone: +61 3 9761 3400

#391
Cafe Saporo
Cuisines: Café
Average Price: Inexpensive
Area: Melbourne
Address: 380 St Kilda Rd
Melbourne Victoria 3000
Phone: +61 3 9696 9974

#392
Dessert House Eatery
Cuisines: Desserts, Café, Asian Fusion
Average Price: Inexpensive
Area: Melbourne
Address: 313 Swanston St
Melbourne Victoria 3000
Phone: +61 3 9663 2284

#393
Ed's Food Hut
Cuisines: Fast Food
Average Price: Inexpensive
Area: Melbourne
Address: 399 Bourke St
Melbourne Victoria 3000
Phone: +61 3 9642 2643

#394
Le Bangkok
Cuisines: Thai
Average Price: Modest
Area: Melbourne
Address: 195 Lonsdale St
Melbourne Victoria 3000
Phone: +61 3 9663 0360

#395
Sushi Monger
Cuisines: Sushi Bar, Japanese
Average Price: Inexpensive
Area: Melbourne
Address: 309 Bourke St
Melbourne Victoria 3000
Phone: +61 3 9663 0899

#396
Stax
Cuisines: Café
Average Price: Inexpensive
Area: Melbourne
Address: 16 Little Latrobe St
Melbourne Victoria 3000
Phone: +61 3 9663 3008

#397
Zam Zam
Cuisines: Indian
Average Price: Modest
Area: Melbourne
Address: 364 Lonsdale St
Melbourne Victoria 3000
Phone: +61 3 9606 0109

#398
Squisito Bar
Cuisines: Café, Italian
Average Price: Inexpensive
Area: Melbourne
Address: 24 Artemis La
Melbourne Victoria 3000
Phone: +61 3 9654 1544

#399
Dessert Story
Cuisines: Desserts, Chinese
Average Price: Inexpensive
Area: Melbourne
Address: 195 Little Bourke St
Melbourne Victoria 3000
Phone: +61 3 9650 7776

#400
Dikstein's Corner Bar
Cuisines: Bar, Pizza
Average Price: Inexpensive
Area: Melbourne
Address: Cnr Bank Place And Little
Collins St Melbourne Victoria 3000
Phone: +61 9 6420 943

#401
Chaf's Cafe
Cuisines: Café
Average Price: Inexpensive
Area: Melbourne
Address: 669 Bourke St
Melbourne Victoria 3000
Phone: +61 3 9629 2296

#402
Meyers Place
Cuisines: Café, Bar
Average Price: Modest
Area: Melbourne
Address: 20 Meyers Pl
Melbourne Victoria 3000
Phone: +61 3 9650 8609

#403
Cafe Victoria
Cuisines: Café
Average Price: Inexpensive
Area: Melbourne
Address: 517 Elizabeth St
Melbourne Victoria 3000
Phone: +61 3 9329 6891

#404
Bellini
Cuisines: Café
Average Price: Modest
Area: Melbourne
Address: 100 Queen St
Melbourne Victoria 3000
Phone: +61 3 9670 0507

#405
Giraffe Cafe
Cuisines: Café, Desserts, Asian Fusion
Average Price: Modest
Area: Melbourne
Address: 302 Little Lonsdale St
Melbourne Victoria 3000
Phone: +61 3 9640 0889

#406
Nick's Bar
Cuisines: Italian
Average Price: Modest
Area: Melbourne
Address: 207 Queen St
Melbourne Victoria 3000
Phone: +61 9 6704 506

#407
Dhaka Restaurant
Cuisines: Indian, Bangladeshi
Average Price: Inexpensive
Area: Melbourne
Address: 145 Lonsdale St
Melbourne Victoria 3000
Phone: +61 3 9654 8109

#408
Paris End Cafe
Cuisines: Café
Average Price: Inexpensive
Area: Melbourne
Address: 20 Collins St
Melbourne Victoria 3000
Phone: +61 3 9654 6138

Melbourne Restaurant Guide / Restaurants, Bars & Cafés

#409
KCL
Cuisines: Café
Average Price: Inexpensive
Area: Melbourne
Address: Ground 389 Flinders Lane
Melbourne Victoria 3000
Phone: +61 3 9620 0360

#410
Noodle Kingdom
Cuisines: Chinese
Average Price: Modest
Area: Melbourne
Address: 264 Swanston St
Melbourne Victoria 3000
Phone: +61 3 9650 1818

#411
Simply Spanish
Cuisines: Tapas, Spanish
Average Price: Modest
Area: Melbourne
Address: 555 Bourke St
Melbourne Victoria 3000
Phone: +61 3 9620 3332

#412
Sushi Hotaru
Cuisines: Australian
Average Price: Modest
Area: Melbourne
Address: 157 Spring St
Melbourne Victoria 3000
Phone: +61 3 9654 0811

#413
The Old Chamber
Cuisines: Café
Average Price: Modest
Area: Melbourne
Address: 395 Collins St
Melbourne Victoria 3000
Phone: +61 3 9999 9999

#414
Han Guuk Gwan
Cuisines: Korean, Chinese
Average Price: Inexpensive
Area: Melbourne
Address: 13 Victoria St
Melbourne Victoria 3000
Phone: +61 3 9639 1747

#415
Rice 'N' Rolls
Cuisines: Fast Food
Average Price: Inexpensive
Area: Melbourne
Address: 181 William St
Melbourne Victoria 3000
Phone: +61 3 9642 2429

#416
Health Express
Cuisines: Fast Food
Average Price: Modest
Area: Melbourne
Address: Spencer St
Melbourne Victoria 3000
Phone: +61 3 8689 7636

#417
Roll'd
Cuisines: Vietnamese
Average Price: Modest
Area: Melbourne
Address: 45 Collins St
Melbourne Victoria 3000
Phone: +61 3 9650 6339

#418
CJ Lunch Bar
Cuisines: Korean
Average Price: Inexpensive
Area: Melbourne
Address: Shop 2 391 Lt Lonsdale St
Melbourne Victoria 3000
Phone: +61 3 9602 5559

#419
Paco's Tacos
Cuisines: Mexican
Average Price: Modest
Area: Melbourne
Address: 500 Bourke St
Melbourne Victoria 3000
Phone: +61 3 9663 3038

#420
Pearson & Murphy's Cafe
Cuisines: Café
Average Price: Modest
Area: Melbourne
Address: 124 La Trobe St
Melbourne Victoria 3000
Phone: +61 3 9639 2777

#421
Ume Hana
Cuisines: Japanese, Korean
Average Price: Modest
Area: Melbourne
Address: 398 Elizabeth St
Melbourne Victoria 3000
Phone: +61 3 9663 1108

#422
Melbourne Bornga
Cuisines: Korean
Average Price: Inexpensive
Area: Melbourne
Address: 258 Lonsdale St
Melbourne Victoria 3000
Phone: +61 3 9663 1112

#423
The Jarrah Room
Cuisines: Restaurant
Average Price: Modest
Area: Melbourne
Address: 44 Spencer St
Melbourne Victoria 3000
Phone: +61 3 9629 5255

#424
Bluebag
Cuisines: Café, Caterer, Health Market
Average Price: Modest
Area: Melbourne
Address: 405 Collins St
Melbourne Victoria 3000
Phone: +61 3 9614 7277

#425
O-Bento
Cuisines: Sushi Bar, Japanese
Average Price: Inexpensive
Area: Melbourne
Address: 210 La Trobe St
Melbourne Victoria 3000
Phone: +61 3 9663 3323

#426
G2 Korean BBQ
Cuisines: Korean
Average Price: Inexpensive
Area: Melbourne
Address: 301 Elizabeth St
Melbourne Victoria 3000
Phone: +61 3 9642 3424

#427
Lustre Bar
Cuisines: Café, Bar
Average Price: Modest
Area: Melbourne
Address: 252 Flinders L & Centre Pl
Melbourne Victoria 3000
Phone: +61 3 9671 3371

#428
Fancy Fillings
Cuisines: Fast Food
Average Price: Modest
Area: Melbourne
Address: Spencer St
Melbourne Victoria 3000
Phone: +61 3 9670 1378

#429
Gopal's Vegetarian Restaurant
Cuisines: Vegetarian, Vegan, Ethnic Food
Average Price: Modest
Area: Melbourne
Address: 139 Swanston St
Melbourne Victoria 3000
Phone: +61 3 9650 1578

#430
Saigon Inn Restaurant
Cuisines: Vietnamese
Average Price: Modest
Area: Melbourne
Address: 11 Liverpool St
Melbourne Victoria 3000
Phone: +61 3 9639 0693

#431
The Tea Salon
Cuisines: Café, Tea Room
Average Price: Modest
Area: Melbourne
Address: Level 2, 295 Lonsdale St
Melbourne Victoria 3000
Phone: +61 3 8609 8188

#432
Korchi City
Cuisines: Korean
Average Price: Modest
Area: Melbourne
Address: 441 Little Bourke St
Melbourne Victoria 3000
Phone: +61 3 9041 0775

#433
Tower Sushi
Cuisines: Sushi Bar, Japanese, Fast Food
Average Price: Inexpensive
Area: Melbourne
Address: 207 Flinders St
Melbourne Victoria 3000
Phone: +61 3 9620 2060

#434
Kanda Sushi Noodle Bar
Cuisines: Sushi Bar, Fast Food
Average Price: Inexpensive
Area: Melbourne
Address: 335 La Trobe St
Melbourne Victoria 3000
Phone: +61 3 9670 0336

#435
Alluvial
Cuisines: Restaurant
Average Price: Expensive
Area: Melbourne
Address: 495 Collins St
Melbourne Victoria 3000
Phone: +61 3 8627 1567

#436
Issara Thai
Cuisines: Thai, Fast Food
Average Price: Inexpensive
Area: Melbourne
Address: 422-428 Little Collins St
Melbourne Victoria 3000
Phone: +61 4 3377 6744

#437
Curry Point
Cuisines: Indian
Average Price: Modest
Area: Melbourne
Address: 392 Bourke St
Melbourne Victoria 3000
Phone: +61 3 9602 2550

#438
Man Tong Kitchen
Cuisines: Chinese
Average Price: Expensive
Area: Melbourne
Address: Level 1, West End
Melbourne Victoria 3006
Phone: +61 3 9686 9888

#439
Chocolate Buddha
Cuisines: Sushi Bar, Japanese
Average Price: Modest
Area: Melbourne
Address: Cnr Swanston St & Flinders St
Melbourne Victoria 3000
Phone: +61 3 9654 5688

#440
Florentino Grossi
Cuisines: Café, Italian, Mediterranean
Average Price: Expensive
Area: Melbourne
Address: 80 Bourke St
Melbourne Victoria 3000
Phone: +61 3 9662 1811

#441
Active Caffe Torre
Cuisines: Café
Average Price: Modest
Area: Melbourne
Address: Shp156/ 211 La Trobe St
Melbourne Victoria 3000
Phone: +61 3 9663 5884

#442
Cafe Brown Sugar
Cuisines: Café
Average Price: Modest
Area: Melbourne
Address: 25 Block Pl
Melbourne Victoria 3000
Phone: +61 3 9639 3933

#443
Nandos
Cuisines: Fast Food
Average Price: Modest
Area: Melbourne
Address: 400 Little Bourke St
Melbourne Victoria 3000
Phone: +61 3 9619 1544

#444
Lorca
Cuisines: Café, Spanish
Average Price: Modest
Area: Melbourne
Address: 7 Centre Pl
Melbourne Victoria 3000
Phone: +61 3 9650 6337

#445
Taco Bill Mexican Restaurants
Cuisines: Mexican
Average Price: Modest
Area: Melbourne
Address: 412 Collins St
Melbourne Victoria 3000
Phone: +61 3 9670 4327

#446
Anju Restaurant & Bar
Cuisines: Korean, Asian Fusion
Average Price: Modest
Area: Melbourne
Address: 18 Little La Trobe St
Melbourne Victoria 3000
Phone: +61 3 9662 4568

#447
Cafenatics On Latrobe
Cuisines: Café
Average Price: Inexpensive
Area: Melbourne
Address: 414 Latrobe St
Melbourne Victoria 3000
Phone: +61 3 9642 4684

#448
Breadtop
Cuisines: Bakery, Chinese, Desserts
Average Price: Inexpensive
Area: Melbourne
Address: Shop 1-2, 200 Bourke St
Melbourne Victoria 3000
Phone: +61 3 9671 3788

#449
Le Croissant Des Halles
Cuisines: Bakery, Breakfast & Brunch
Average Price: Inexpensive
Area: Melbourne
Address: 507 Elizabeth St
Melbourne Victoria 3000
Phone: +61 3 9328 4752

#450
Church Of Secular Coffee
Cuisines: Coffee, Tea, Burgers
Average Price: Inexpensive
Area: Melbourne
Address: 80 Collins St
Melbourne Victoria 3000
Phone: +61 3 9686 2990

#451
Shoya
Cuisines: Sushi Bar, Japanese
Average Price: Exclusive
Area: Melbourne
Address: 25 Market Ln
Melbourne Victoria 3000
Phone: +61 3 9650 0848

#452
Hopetoun Tea Room
Cuisines: Café
Average Price: Modest
Area: Melbourne
Address: Shop 1 & 2 282 Collins St
Melbourne Victoria 3000
Phone: +61 3 9650 2777

#453
Cafe Tono Pizza Pasta Bar
Cuisines: Italian, Pizza
Average Price: Modest
Area: Melbourne
Address: 181 Bourke St
Melbourne Victoria 3000
Phone: +61 3 9650 3379

#454
Medallion Cafe Souvlaki & Cakes
Cuisines: Café, Greek
Average Price: Modest
Area: Melbourne
Address: 211 Lonsdale St
Melbourne Victoria 3000
Phone: +61 3 9663 4228

#455
Your Thai
Cuisines: Thai
Average Price: Inexpensive
Area: Melbourne
Address: 255 Swanston St
Melbourne Victoria 3000
Phone: +61 3 9663 8010

#456
Itoya Cafe
Cuisines: Ethnic Food, Japanese
Average Price: Inexpensive
Area: Melbourne
Address: 200 Spencer St
Melbourne Victoria 3000
Phone: +61 3 9078 5268

#457
Sushi Sushi
Cuisines: Japanese, Sushi Bar
Average Price: Modest
Area: Melbourne
Address: 148 Swanston St
Melbourne Victoria 3000
Phone: +61 3 9650 6880

#458
Jalan Alor
Cuisines: Malaysian
Average Price: Modest
Area: Melbourne
Address: 7/206 Bourke St,
Melbourne Victoria 3000
Phone: +61 3 9663 1138

#459
Siglo
Cuisines: Wine Bar, Lounge, Gastropub
Average Price: Modest
Area: Melbourne
Address: 161 Spring St
Melbourne Victoria 3000
Phone: +61 3 9654 6631

#460
Big Mama
Cuisines: Korean
Average Price: Modest
Area: Carlton
Address: 466 Swanston St
Melbourne Victoria 3053
Phone: +61 3 9347 2656

#461
Locanda Restaurant & Bar
Cuisines: Italian
Average Price: Modest
Area: Melbourne
Address: 186 Exhibition St
Melbourne Victoria 3000
Phone: +61 3 9635 1246

#462
Supper Inn
Cuisines: Chinese
Average Price: Modest
Area: Melbourne
Address: 15 Celestial Ave
Melbourne Victoria 3000
Phone: +61 3 9663 4759

#463
Donburi And BBQ
Cuisines: Korean, Japanese
Average Price: Modest
Area: Melbourne
Address: 108 Bourke St,
Melbourne Victoria 3000
Phone: +61 3 9663 3013

#464
Onni Cafe
Cuisines: Café
Average Price: Inexpensive
Area: Melbourne
Address: 472 Little Lonsdale St
Melbourne Victoria 3000
Phone: +61 3 9642 8032

#465
De La France
Cuisines: Caterer, French
Average Price: Inexpensive
Area: Melbourne
Address: 247 Bourke St
Melbourne Victoria 3000
Phone: +61 3 9663 0255

#466
Melbourne Pizza Bar
Cuisines: Italian, Pizza
Average Price: Modest
Area: Melbourne
Address: 181 King St
Melbourne Victoria 3000
Phone: +61 3 9670 5314

#467
Dognation Causeway
Cuisines: Hot Dogs
Average Price: Inexpensive
Area: Melbourne
Address: Shop 2
Melbourne Victoria 3000
Phone: +61 4 2308 3287

#468
Nashi CBW
Cuisines: Café
Average Price: Inexpensive
Area: Melbourne
Address: TG11/ 181 William St
Melbourne Victoria 3000
Phone: +61 3 9606 0126

#469
Syracuse Restaurant
Cuisines: Restaurant
Average Price: Expensive
Area: Melbourne
Address: 23 Bank Place
Melbourne Victoria 3000
Phone: +61 3 9670 1777

#470
Gong De Lin
Cuisines: Shanghainese,
Vegetarian, Vegan
Average Price: Inexpensive
Area: Melbourne
Address: 264 Swanston St
Melbourne Victoria 3000
Phone: +61 3 9663 7878

#471
The Cupcake Family
Cuisines: Bakery, Café
Average Price: Modest
Area: Melbourne
Address: Shop22, Red Cape Ln
Melbourne Victoria 3000
Phone: +61 3 9663 0055

#472
Sun Asia
Cuisines: Chinese
Average Price: Inexpensive
Area: Melbourne
Address: Shp27/ 190 Lonsdale St
Melbourne Victoria 3000
Phone: +61 3 9663 8178

#473
Mr Kitchen
Cuisines: Vietnamese
Average Price: Inexpensive
Area: Melbourne
Address: 319 Swanston St
Melbourne Victoria 3000
Phone: +61 4 2146 46351

#474
Bing Boy Melbourne Central
Cuisines: Street Vendor, Asian Fusion, Sandwiches
Average Price: Inexpensive
Area: Melbourne
Address: 211 Latrobe St
Melbourne Victoria 3000
Phone: +61 3 9922 1100

#475
The Khan Mongolian BBQ
Cuisines: Mongolian
Average Price: Modest
Area: Melbourne
Address: 295 Exhibition St
Melbourne Victoria 3000
Phone: +61 3 9663 7477

#476
Gifts @ CQ
Cuisines: Buffet
Average Price: Inexpensive
Area: Melbourne
Address: 418 Little Collins St
Melbourne Victoria 3000
Phone: +61 3 8601 2760

#477
Captains Of Industry
Cuisines: Café,
Average Price: Modest
Area: Melbourne
Address: 2 Somerset Pl
Melbourne Victoria 3000
Phone: +61 3 9670 4405

#478
Ajisen Ramen
Cuisines: Japanese, Chinese
Average Price: Modest
Area: Melbourne
Address: 130 Bourke St
Melbourne Victoria 3000
Phone: +61 3 9662 1100

#479
Kun Ming
Cuisines: Chinese
Average Price: Modest
Area: Melbourne
Address: 212 Little Bourke St
Melbourne Victoria 3000
Phone: +61 3 9663 1851

#480
Jolly J's Curry Shack
Cuisines: Restaurant
Average Price: Inexpensive
Area: Melbourne
Address: 232 Flinders St
Melbourne Victoria 3000
Phone: +61 3 9650 9989

#481
Punjabi Curry Cafe
Cuisines: Indian
Average Price: Modest
Area: Collingwood
Address: 87 Johnston St
Melbourne Victoria 3066
Phone: +61 3 9419 5307

#482
Panned Pizza
Cuisines: Mediterranean, Food, Fast Food
Average Price: Inexpensive
Area: Melbourne
Address: 189 - 191 Bourke St
Melbourne Victoria 3000
Phone: +61 3 9663 6339

#483
Cafe L'Incontro
Cuisines: Café, Coffee, Tea, Italian
Average Price: Modest
Area: Melbourne
Address: Cnr Little Collins St
& Swanston St Melbourne Victoria 3000
Phone: +61 3 9650 9603

#484
Kaneda Japanese Restaurant
Cuisines: Japanese
Average Price: Modest
Area: Melbourne
Address: 200 Bourke St Shop 6
Melbourne Victoria 3000
Phone: +61 3 9663 8802

#485
Spaghetti Tree
Cuisines: Italian
Average Price: Modest
Area: Melbourne
Address: 59 Bourke St
Melbourne Victoria 3000
Phone: +61 3 9650 3174

#486
N Lee Bakery
Cuisines: Café, Vietnamese, Bakery
Average Price: Inexpensive
Area: Melbourne
Address: 62 Little Collins St
Melbourne Victoria 3000
Phone: +61 3 9419 9732

#487
Morgans At 401
Cuisines: Venues, Event Space, Breakfast & Brunch
Average Price: Modest
Area: Melbourne
Address: 401 Collins St
Melbourne Victoria 3000
Phone: +61 3 9223 2413

#488
Takumi
Cuisines: Karaoke, Teppanyaki
Average Price: Expensive
Area: Melbourne
Address: 32 Bourke St
Melbourne Victoria 3000
Phone: +61 3 9650 7020

#489
Melbourne Central Lion Hotel
Cuisines: British, Pub, Lounge
Average Price: Modest
Area: Melbourne
Address: 211 La Trobe St
Melbourne Victoria 3000
Phone: +61 3 9663 5977

#490
Kay'z Cafe
Cuisines: Breakfast & Brunch, Fast Food
Average Price: Inexpensive
Area: Melbourne
Address: 595 Elizabeth St
Melbourne Victoria 3000
Phone: +61 3 9328 5111

#491
Pie Face
Cuisines: Bakery, Café, Fast Food
Average Price: Inexpensive
Area: Melbourne
Address: 270 Swanston St
Melbourne Victoria 3000
Phone: +61 3 9662 2240

#492
Golden Orchids Malaysian Restaurant
Cuisines: Malaysian
Average Price: Modest
Area: Melbourne
Address: 126 Lit Bourke St
Melbourne Victoria 3000
Phone: +61 3 9663 1101

#493
Dumpling Noodle House
Cuisines: Chinese
Average Price: Inexpensive
Area: Melbourne
Address: 210 Lonsdale St
Melbourne Victoria 3000
Phone: +61 3 9654 7388

#494
Oporto
Cuisines: Chicken Shop, Fast Food, Burgers
Average Price: Inexpensive
Area: Melbourne
Address: 210 Lonsdale St
Melbourne Victoria 3000
Phone: +61 3 9654 6366

#495
Ramen Ya
Cuisines: Ramen
Average Price: Inexpensive
Area: Melbourne
Address: 269 Lonsdale St
Melbourne Victoria 3000
Phone: +61 3 8609 8174

#496
New Shanghai
Cuisines: Shanghainese
Average Price: Inexpensive
Area: Melbourne
Address: 287 Lonsdale St
Melbourne Victoria 3000
Phone: +61 3 9994 9386

#497
Yami Yami
Cuisines: Korean, Japanese
Average Price: Inexpensive
Area: Melbourne
Address: 398 Lonsdale St
Melbourne Victoria 3000
Phone: +61 3 9670 3323

#498
Sofitel Melbourne On Collins
Cuisines: Venues, Event Space, Hotel, Restaurant
Average Price: Exclusive
Area: Melbourne
Address: 25 Collins St
Melbourne Victoria 3000
Phone: +61 3 9653 0000

#499
Golden Tower
Cuisines: Burgers, American, Café
Average Price: Modest
Area: Melbourne
Address: 145 Swanston St
Melbourne Victoria 3000
Phone: +61 3 9650 9237

#500
China Bar
Cuisines: Chinese
Average Price: Inexpensive
Area: Melbourne
Address: 235 Russell St
Melbourne Victoria 3000
Phone: +61 3 9639 7012

Printed in Great Britain
by Amazon